Becoming Self-Made

THE JOURNEY OF BUILDING A SOUL-LED MULTIMILLION-DOLLAR BUSINESS

Here's to having it ALL!
♥ Elaina Ray

Copyright @ 2022 Elaina Ray
Becoming Self-Made: The Journey of Building a Soul-Led Multimillion-Dollar Business
YGTMedia Co. Trade Paperback Edition.
ISBN trade paperback: 978-1-989716-71-7
eBook: 978-1-989716-72-4
Audio Book: 978-1-989716-73-1

All Rights Reserved. No part of this book can be scanned, distributed, or copied without permission. This book or any portion thereof may not be reproduced or used in any manner whatsoever without the express written permission of the publisher at publishing@ygtmedia.co—except for the use of brief quotations in a book review.

The author has made every effort to ensure the accuracy of the information within this book was correct at time of publication. The author does not assume and hereby disclaims any liability to any party for any loss, damage, or disruption caused by errors or omissions, whether such errors or omissions result from accident, negligence, or any other cause.

This book is designed to provide information and motivation to our readers. It is sold with the understanding that the publisher is not engaged to render any type of psychological, legal, or any other kind of professional advice. The content is the sole expression and opinion of its author, and not necessarily that of the publisher. No warranties or guarantees are expressed or implied by the publisher's choice to include any of the content in this book. Neither the publisher nor the author shall be liable for any physical, psychological, emotional, financial, or commercial damages, including, but not limited to, special, incidental, consequential or other damages. Our views and rights are the same: You are responsible for your own choices, actions, and results.

Published in Canada, for Global Distribution by YGTMedia Co.

www.ygtmedia.co/publishing

To order additional copies of this book: publishing@ygtmedia.co

Developmental editing by Tania Jane Moraes-Vaz
Edited by Christine Stock
Book design by Doris Chung
Cover design by Michelle Fairbanks
ePub edition by Ellie Silpa
Author Photo by Herry Santosa

TORONTO

Becoming Self-Made

THE JOURNEY OF BUILDING A SOUL-LED MULTIMILLION-DOLLAR BUSINESS

ELAINA RAY

DEDICATION

To my parents who shaped me, supported me, and gave me the wonderful raw material to work with to become who I am today. I am forever grateful.

To Bali, for allowing me to make my home here. I bow onto this land, give thanks, and offer my humble prayers for the grace and healing this place has shown me.

To any man or woman out there who doubts their ability to become self-made, autonomous, and powerful, this is for you.

To the millions of emerging entrepreneurs: I can't wait to see what you create and how the world changes as you turn heads and bring massive value and positive influence to us all.

TABLE OF CONTENTS

	PREFACE	4
	INTRODUCTION	10
1	HONORING YOUR SOUL-KNOWING AND LISTENING FOR NUDGES (OR SHOVES) IN THE RIGHT DIRECTION	30
2	DROPSHIPPING T-SHIRTS OR DOING MY SOUL WORK?	44
3	MY FIRST $100,000 IDEA	55
4	THE BREAKDOWN BEFORE THE BREAKTHROUGH: MY HEALING JOURNEY	66
5	THE DAY I MET MY FIRST COACH AND QUIT HOARDING MY ACORNS	78
6	PRESSING PLAY	95
7	FALLING IN LOVE	116
8	CASTING OFF FROM MY VERY LAST JOB (AND FINDING SAFETY WITHIN)	127
9	LEADING YOURSELF THROUGH THE UNKNOWN: THE YEARS WHERE EVERYTHING SHIFTED	137
10	GOING ALL IN	149

11	MAKING EXPANSIVE FINANCIAL DECISIONS AND WIELDING YOUR ECONOMIC POWER	162
12	THE FEMININE ENERGY INITIATION AND BUILDING MY DREAM TEAM	180
13	GETTING IT "RIGHT": THE 1 PERCENT SHIFT FROM GREAT TO EXTRAORDINARY	197
14	BECOMING SELF-MADE FROM THE INSIDE OUT: A HEALTH REFORMATION	218
15	UNDERSTANDING THE PARADOX OF GROWTH	232
16	HEARTBREAK, LOSS, AND COMING UNDONE	244
17	THE ART OF RECEIVING MORE	260
18	LOCKING IN CONSISTENCY IN YOUR BUSINESS	277
19	BUSTING MYTHS AND STORIES PEOPLE TELL ABOUT BUSINESS THAT JUST AREN'T TRUE	295
	CONCLUSION	325
	ACKNOWLEDGMENTS	335
	RESOURCES & WORKS CITED	340

PREFACE

This book is dedicated to the version of me who left everything behind and moved to Bali with a calling in her heart. The twenty-nine-year-old who lived in a moldy $400/month bungalow in Ubud for a year trying desperately to figure it out, who believed she had to do it all on her own.

I am writing to her, telling her all the things I know now that I wish I would have known then.

Back then, I only knew that I couldn't go back. I couldn't work for someone else again. I couldn't work to save up, quit my job, travel the world and finally feel alive until the money ran out, and then do it all over again. The cycle was exhausting.

Back then, I didn't see myself as an entrepreneur. My goal was to be a freelancer and to be able to piece together enough sources of income to keep me out of the nine-to-five. Fundamentally, I was in survival mode. The bar was set to "just make enough to stay free and stay alive," so it was always a struggle. In many ways, I was addicted to the struggle.

Becoming a millionaire never really crossed my mind, or if it did, it seemed like something I might accomplish in my old age, maybe before I died.

The momentum my business took on shortly after the winter of 2019 blindsided me and everyone in my life.

The before and after snapshots of me in the winter of 2019 and me writing this book now in the fall of 2021 are hilarious.

BEFORE: DECEMBER 2018, AGE: 29

LOCATION: one-bedroom bungalow with not so much as even a desk or a sofa. Rent: $400/month
STATE OF MIND: scrambling, desperate, isolated, confused
RELATIONSHIP STATUS: single
JOB: part-time freelancer for an online matchmaking company making $100 for every date I set up, part-time freelance writer for an online travel magazine that paid $150/article, part-time "coach" making $90/hour for one-off sessions from a single page on my blog that had a trickle of web traffic, and very part-time yoga teacher at the local yoga shala twice per week
DAILY ACTIVITIES: chanting the *gayatri* mantra at 7 a.m., praying to God for a man and a client or two to pay my rent, deciding whether I could afford a smoothie AND a salad for lunch (or just the salad), sitting in cafés sipping a single lukewarm caffe latte while "working"
NET WORTH: $15,000

AFTER: SEPTEMBER 2021, AGE: 31

LOCATION: six-bedroom dream villa (which I own) with an Olympic-sized swimming pool, sauna, and gym

STATE OF MIND: peaceful, creative, abundant, focused, grateful

RELATIONSHIP STATUS: taken by a committed, beautiful man sent to me by angels

JOB: seven-figure coach, success mentor, and business strategist to some of the top coaches, personal development experts, healers, and brands on the internet today

DAILY ACTIVITIES: sleep in, cuddle with my man and small family of cats, manage my team, take one or two calls for the world-class masterminds I run, write this book, stare at the screen while trying to write this book, spend time with friends, get paid to read and learn and come up with new ideas

NET WORTH: $2M+

At twenty-nine, I was still a child in many ways, running away from home and responsibility, sitting on a yoga mat chanting to Ganesha in cheap clothes purchased in the markets of northern India, riddled with scoliosis, gut, and mommy issues, and utterly ignorant of my brilliance, worth, and potential.

By thirty-one, I had claimed my throne as a woman and as a confident entrepreneur. I became a self-made millionaire, international real estate investor, and loving partner to an incredible man.

This book will take you on the journey of what had to happen for this huge quantum leap to occur in the span of only two years. I will share with you everything I wish I had known back when I was duct-taping pieces of my life back together after leaving a stable corporate career, surviving a spiritual awakening, and moving across the world to build my future with only a few thousand dollars in the bank and the vaguest sense of what it might look like.

The fact that I've wound up where I am today is nothing short of a miracle . . .

. . . and the product of many moments when I walked to the edge of the abyss in my life and stared into the unknown, knowing that either wild entrepreneurial success or utter financial ruin lie ahead.

Peering over the edge into complete blackness,
I leapt.
Trusting my calling, trusting that I couldn't go back.

There were many, many flying leaps into darkness over the years.

I wouldn't be here today if I was still standing on the edge of The Void, calculating all the potential ways it could go wrong or waiting, hoping, praying for someone to come along and go first and show me that it was safe.

You've picked up this book because you have a calling as well.

Maybe it's clear and you're already well on your way to making a magnificent contribution to the world through your business, or maybe up until now it's simply been a faint sense of leadership, creation, and pioneering of some kind that stirs within you.

To realize your dream, there's no way around the fact that you must also walk to the edge of your own personal abyss and swan dive into the unknown that awaits you.

This book is meant to help you leap, to quicken your results, and to soften the landing.

It means the world to me to be able to share with you the wisdom I've accrued while navigating a portal of such massive transformation and expansion myself, landing with feet firmly planted on the other side of all those wild leaps of faith.

INTRODUCTION

ROME, ITALY
SEPTEMBER 18, 2012

There's a distinct sound an Italian ambulance makes.

It's more of a subtle rising and falling crescendo, like "WEE-ow, WEE-ow," rather than the American one that sounds like a steady, shrill, murderous cry of "WAAAAAAAAAAAAH."

I felt my stomach drop. I was perched in a tiny back alley of Rome with a smorgasbord of freshly sliced prosciutto and melon, a lightly tossed spaghetti, and a glass of chenin blanc sitting on the table next to my laptop where I begrudgingly listened to an IBM financial services conference call. I was about to give my update on an internal strategy project based out of New York City.

Rrrrrright. New York City, where I was supposed to be. Where all my colleagues thought I was working from home in my tiny Manhattan apartment, a room in the East Village that I shared with a friend because I wanted to save money on rent so I could afford experiences like these.

I had slipped away to Italy to "work from home" from Rome, Venice, and Lago di Como for a month, thinking that no one would even notice.

They wouldn't except for the dead giveaway of a European ambulance sound piercing the background of my update, the sketchy Roman Wi-Fi already perhaps a sign that I wasn't in my home office a few miles from any urgent team meeting that might need to take place in person.

I was always up to shenanigans like this.

Nothing created a sicklier feeling in my stomach than the resentment that built up in me as I repeatedly turned away from myself and my true desires and twisted myself into a pretzel to keep a good job for over a year and a half. A job I *should* have been happy to have, that I competed with thousands of other top college graduates to get, a job that paid more in a single year than what both my parents combined made after three decades of hard work.

It's that feeling you get when you're driving at seventy miles per hour down the highway and you realize you just missed your exit—a feeling of bristling annoyance, anxiety, and more than a tiny bit of self-loathing, which continues to build up until you see the next exit.

That was how I felt when I went to ask my bosses for time off at the end of accumulating my first year's worth of vacation—already picturing myself in the Brazilian Amazon—and hearing that I only got two weeks.

Two weeks?! That would barely let me recover from jet leg and get *into* the Amazon, not to mention the multiday excursion I wanted to do by boat into the most remote areas.

This whole job thing was fundamentally in the way of my soul's freedom, my true nature, and the way I envisioned living my life as a devoted world citizen.

But I didn't quit that time. Instead, I planned a month-long trip to Brazil, exactly like I wanted, and parked it right up against the December holidays to extend the uninterrupted vacation time to three weeks (which I affectionately call "corporate vacation Tetris"), then simply decided I would fake being sick for the last week.

And that's what I did. I flew down to Rio at the beginning of December, which is prime time to be on Copacabana Beach, took Portuguese lessons in Salvador, went to street festivals and danced in the favelas with the locals, kissed cute Brazilian boys, and slept in hammocks deep in the Amazon after evenings of spearfishing and stargazing.

One sunrise in Morro de São Paulo, a picturesque, car-free island where tiny caipirinha stalls dot the beach and there's all-night dance parties every night, I sat with a new Israeli friend, Itai, who I met in my hostel, buzzed and more alive than I had felt all year living in New York, and I finally committed to change.

Itai was in the middle of traveling the world for nine months. I was in the middle of another little white lie that I had the flu so I could squeak out seven more days of freedom before returning to another year of the same ol' handcuffs and rationed paychecks. I couldn't keep up the shenanigans. I had to be honest with myself.

I was the young woman who had studied Mandarin for four years in college, the woman who—from the moment she set foot in rural China at nineteen years old and with a short conversation crossed a cultural chasm as deep as the one that should have existed between her and an elderly Chinese woman cooking *chuan'r* on the side of the road in Fujian Province—became hooked into another universe. The dancing colors of Mother Earth, her cultures, her languages, and her people were the things that fascinated me and brought aliveness into my body in a way nothing else ever had.

I went back to New York and changed my ways. I contacted everyone in my network and aggressively applied to every overseas job I could find. Within ninety days, I had flown to Barcelona on a regular weekend, interviewed for and was offered my dream job, accepted it on the spot, and gave my two weeks' notice to my boss at IBM on Monday. I negotiated a start date two months out so I could solo travel through Japan and Taiwan before flying to Lagos, Nigeria, to start my new position as an international project manager for a Spanish media company with outposts in every emerging market country in Asia, the Middle East, and Africa. There, I'd rotate through three-month assignments in places like Ethiopia, Oman, Mongolia, and South Africa. I had created a reality that matched the highest version of my truth and stepped into a living dream.

After the Brazil awakening, I decided to never give my power away again. I would never spin little lies or twist myself into a pretzel to be someone I fundamentally am not ever again. I would never feel my stomach drop the way it did when the ambulance sounded in Italy that afternoon where I thought I'd be caught in my shenanigans, not proud of who I was behind the scenes trying to steal away small snippets of happiness and freedom. At what price?

Since then, I've never again lived in the United States, and I've never again lied for the sake of mere scraps of joy, freedom, and love. I went on to enjoy two years of that dream job, left it to travel the world solo for a year and a half, and landed one more dream job with Uber before my corporate career abruptly ended with the knowing that ultimately, I couldn't work on someone else's clock and receive paycheck rationings that limited my savings, investment, and creative potential—and somehow be happy. We'll get to that momentous, unceremonious kick in the ass shortly.

In short, I went on to become an entrepreneur.

At first, a struggling one, for sure. One who couldn't focus on one thing long enough to get any traction, one who doubted her value outside of a workplace where she excelled at doing what she was told to do, one who couldn't strum up clients, one who didn't attract wild fanfare when she published her first offers, one who would work long hours on products that simply didn't sell.

But eventually, and this book will guide you through the journey, it became easier. I began to understand the marketplace. I hired help. I saw my own gifts and value more clearly. I found focus. And I stayed the course as I began to earn incrementally more money, all of which allowed me to feel more and more secure on this new life path I had chosen: unabashed, uninhibited, unapologetic, uncompromised, and with unlimited freedom.

> I AM HAPPIEST AND TRUEST TO MYSELF WHEN I AM AN UNTETHERED CITIZEN OF THE WORLD, THE CHIEF EXECUTIVE OFFICER OF MY OWN GODDAMN TIME, A MESSENGER FOR THE EVOLUTION OF THE FREEDOM ECONOMY, AND A POWERFUL RESOURCE FOR TENS OF THOUSANDS OF MEN AND WOMEN GLOBALLY WHO WANT TO CREATE THE SAME AUTONOMOUS LIFESTYLE FOR THEMSELVES.

Ultimately, I went the long way around to arrive at the same truth I knew deep down all along: that I am happiest and truest to myself when I am an untethered citizen of the world, the chief executive officer of my own goddamn time, a messenger for the evolution of the freedom economy, and a powerful resource for tens of thousands of men and women globally who want to create the same autonomous lifestyle for themselves.

Well, easier said than done.

It took me about *ten years* to figure all this out because the idea of working for myself and being able to fully support myself with just my natural gifts was incompatible with my upbringing and conditioning. My mom was a Sunday morning coupon clipper and dollar-stretching artist who politely and firmly reminded me to turn off the lights after leaving a room or to put on a sweater inside during the winter so we could reduce the electricity bill. My dad worked in construction for the same company for more than forty years. They are both as blue collar, good hearted, and hard working as they come. The values they instilled in me served me well, yet I hadn't known a single entrepreneur growing up. It was a mystical, uncertain path I had to forge one step at a time, machete in one hand, thrift shop compass in the other.

This book is the journey of me really owning my truth and becoming a self-made woman, and it's about you claiming the throne of your own empire as well.

You don't have ten years. I'd like to save you the time, runaround, and wild goose chase by equipping you with some of the tools that have quantum leaped my success to become the entrepreneur I was always destined to become. Like me back then, you may not have the examples or real-life friends and allies of out-of-the-box entrepreneurial success, so let me be one for you. Let me show you how a girl from the lower-middle-class neighborhoods of Buffalo, New York, can become a self-made millionaire by the age of thirty-one and provide you all the evidence you need to stake your claim to the path of prosperity and sovereignty you and everyone else with a desire like yours burning in the depths of their heart rightly deserve.

I didn't come out of the womb feeling worthy and capable of running my own company. I had to learn to feel capable. I had to invest in myself, teach myself, get myself in rooms with people doing things I felt utterly intimidated by and grow from feeling about two feet tall to being able to command rooms of influencers, leaders, and multimillionaires, make $100,000 months, and lead a team of eight like I do now.

I am a die-hard advocate of you keeping the power of your time, money, and energy in your own hands and making decisions that collapse the time and distance between you and your dreams, whether that be to travel the world, have enough time to spend with your family, write books, become a professional dancer, be a part-time hobby artist, generously support your favorite causes, create space for advanced spiritual practice or personal development, or simply *rest* after the hard work and demanding education you've probably navigated up until now.

It's not my job to dictate what your dreams and desires should be; it's my (self-appointed) job to have you stop wasting time and misjudging the distance and difficulty of the route from where you are now and the lifestyle, abundance, and purpose that's possible for you and every person on this planet.

And I know that the fastest, most straightforward route to you having as much power as possible to direct the course of your life and shape your legacy in any way you want is for you to become self-made. To become someone who runs your own company, makes your own rules, decides your own hours, and receives unlimited amounts of wealth as opposed to rationed amounts of self-directed time, money, and energy.

Studies show that wealth accumulation differs significantly between entrepreneurs and employees.[1] Some will chalk this up to mindset differentiation, but here's what I believe: As long as you allow other people to control how much you can earn, what you can do with your time and energy, and how you get to leverage your numerous talents and skills, you will be at their mercy. Your potential for earning and expression is capped unless you actively choose to leave behind the limiting constraints of the ordinary world of employment and lead a company and movement doing what you were born to do.

I don't believe in paying your dues or receiving an ordinary, incremental amount of money or influence in life. I am a champion of you getting what you want *now* and stepping into the most powerful, capable, high-earning, free, and honest version of yourself *now*. It is a fact that you'll be in the best position to be healthier, live a longer life, help more people, and leave a transgenerational legacy and the wealth to go with it if you're the CEO of your own business. To quote Chris Harder, "When good people make good money, they do great things."

I believe that everyone, including you, has a unique gift they are meant to bring to their communities and the world at large. I believe that gift, without exception, can be monetized so that you never trade unhappy labor for an unhappy dollar but instead get paid to be yourself in the world, sharing your natural-born, God-given genius with others who value, respect, and remunerate your work because it is of unquestionably high service.

I am a champion for a different vision of our economy. Imagine how different the world might look if more people were able to participate not in mere jobs but in vocations that generate and circulate more wealth, more love, more joy, more alignment, more purpose, and more satisfaction that lead to greater health, improved productivity, and more resourced communities.[2]

Judging by the fact that you've picked up this book, I'm guessing that you agree with me and hold that vision as well. Welcome.

Whether you already know you want to be an entrepreneur and you're struggling to figure out how and what you'll do to make it a reality or you're already an existing business owner wanting to scale up, I've got you.

From the time I finally stopped denying my truth and actually started building my own business with earnest intention, I generated one million dollars cash received to my company within just two years—an unprecedented level of growth for a self-run online business.

In my world, I see numerous entrepreneurs achieving this level of success. Still, when compared to the vast majority of entrepreneurs, this exponential growth in wealth and income isn't typical. Statistics show that most businesses fail within the first few years[3] and how few female-owned businesses ever hit seven figures.[4]

It's not up to me to decide how much money you earn or desire to earn in your business. Throughout this book, I will simply challenge you on your ideas of what's possible and present a case for why aiming to become a self-made millionaire is the bare minimum you should set your sights on achieving as you walk this path of entrepreneurship.

Becoming an entrepreneur is no joke. You'll be challenged at a very spiritual and cellular level if you decide to go down this path (or let's be real: decide to wildly succeed on this path because you're no underachiever). You'll be required to confront all your self-limiting beliefs when you relinquish the safety of the paycheck rationing and put yourself out there for anyone and everyone on the internet to judge and potentially reject you. You will heal parts of your heart and psyche you didn't even know were broken and hurting until you ran head-on into them vis-à-vis your money stories when it was time to invest in yourself or your clients suggested you were less than perfect or your product launch completely failed . . . for the third time.

If you're going to go through all that, you might as well be highly paid for it. Am I right?

Entrepreneurship has brought me wealth, and wealth has brought me a whole lot of options. I started writing this book in the stunning, modern villa I own in Bali, Indonesia, and finished it while traveling through Europe and the Middle East. I wrote the introduction between snorkels on a dive boat off the coast of Nusa Lembongan during a one-month break from coaching work. I was swimming with gigantic rainbow fish and swirling, pulsing pink corals before telling my partner, "Babe, I just downloaded the entire introduction to the book. I've got to go scribble down the outline. Be right back!" (and he just rolled his eyes at his crazy girlfriend honoring her creative genius ever bubbling up to the surface!).

I take client calls from anywhere in the world and run my now multi-seven-figure business in about fifteen to twenty hours per week, which leaves a lot of time for writing books, investing in real estate, attending personal development retreats, supporting organizations that help develop local Balinese entrepreneurs and reduce poverty on the island, and generally following my bliss.

After growing up wearing secondhand clothes and not being able to afford Abercrombie T-shirts like the cool girls, having a personal stylist and being able to shop for clothing without looking at the price tags is one of my inner goddess's dreams. After growing up ashamed about having the wealthier kids from school over to my small house and then traveling nomadically around the world with just two suitcases of simple belongings, I now love hosting networking events, celebrations, and fundraisers in my beautiful home. I even chose to hire an interior decorator to help make it my ultimate creative sanctuary. I've created dozens of jobs for other self-made people who love what they do, from interior designers to villa managers, copywriters, cooks, and web designers. Money comes in and money goes out, circulating in a micro-economy I've created by owning up to my potential.

I can support my partner's dreams, help my family, and be generous with friends. I can shop at Louis Vuitton and know I can afford anything in the store. I can set aside tens of thousands of dollars into long-term investments and places where every dollar goes to work creating more dollars every day inside my portfolio. I can walk into a house and decide I want to buy it . . . and then buy it. I can use the freedom of my time and energy to support people like you, tens of thousands of you in fact, to emancipate yourselves from any false sense of restriction, smallness, unworthiness, and conditioned attachment to mediocrity so you can have more options to serve bigger, experience more simple day-to-day joys like waking up without an alarm clock, and influence the world around you as you personally see fit.

Note: Whenever people try to tell me what to do with my business, money, or time, I respond with something like "What a beautiful idea. I invite you to go build your own company (in fact, you may want to hire me to help you with that), make your own millions, become the man or woman able to hold it all sustainably and reliably, and make those exact very worthwhile contributions and decisions for yourself. I'll be over here managing my platform and influencing the world the way I desire, because I've earned it." Feel free to borrow any part of that statement when someone tries to push their ideas of what you should do with your time or money on you.

The whole point is to give you the choice to do with your life what you desire, and the fullest extent of that possibility only opens up when you're in the driver's seat 100 percent of the time with 100 percent of your money and 100 percent ownership of your own little money-printing factory (a.k.a. your own business that monetizes your gifts).

Overall, options feel great and are certainly one of the biggest tangible reasons I want to support you to become self-made and in charge of more money and, subsequently, more influence. You'll do good things with it. You'll do what you desire with it, and your desires, whatever they are, are worthy and safe guidance.

But ultimately, entrepreneurship has metamorphosed me from a scared little girl in a never-ending purgatory of one nine-to-five job after another, shaken and unsure of herself, to a powerful woman who cast off the ties to the illusion of safety, healed herself of any idea of smallness and politeness, accepted her inappropriate level of ambition and desire, and decided to take up some space.

And charge for it handsomely.

> IT WAS COMMITTING TO LEARNING HOW TO BECOME A BETTER BUSINESS OWNER DAY BY DAY AND DOING IT ANYWAY, IMPERFECTLY, THAT LED ME TO SIMULTANEOUSLY UNEARTH AND REARRANGE PARTS OF MYSELF THAT NEEDED UPGRADING IN ORDER TO ACHIEVE THE NEXT NEAREST MILESTONE.

Entrepreneurship has been the ultimate healing journey for me. It has been spiritual. Wholesome. Humbling and exhilarating. And it wasn't that I needed to first heal myself completely and become perfectly aligned and have zero remaining limiting beliefs before I could step into being a successful business owner. Far from it, in fact. It was committing to learning *how* to become a better business owner day by day and doing it anyway, imperfectly, that led me to simultaneously unearth and rearrange parts of myself that needed upgrading in order to achieve the next nearest milestone.

I moved little milestone by little milestone, little intuitive hit by little intuitive hit. I got my first hundred-dollar client. I set up a basic website by myself. I got another client. I made my first Facebook post offering my services. I hired my first coach to teach me about online marketing. I learned to hold a sales call. I heard "no" a dozen times until I heard the one "yes" I needed. I paid my rent by the skin of my teeth. I asked for help from peers a little further ahead in the game. I mastered making $10,000 long before I made a million.

I invite you to do the same. Move one imperfect step at a time and move before you're ready. Ready is a myth. The choice to do it now and to do it anyway and to do it because you're called is the path of the entrepreneur who will move mountains with his or her work.

Let this book be your guide. This book will take you through that journey with me and share with you the pieces of wisdom and tangible practices I wished I had known when I first embarked on the journey of becoming self-made. I want your journey to be easier and faster than mine. We don't have time to waste to get your work out into the world. It is needed. Your voice is essential.

Your voice will attract a segment of the market right now that doesn't know what it's missing until they see you and hear you and then they will migrate right over and become raving fans. They'll buy everything you sell. They'll tell their friends about you. They'll read your emails and genuinely care about what you have to share. They'll respond to you when you're in need like you're a member of their family. Their lives will change from the things you do and share with them. They'll be wowed by the value you bring to the table. They'll be your soul community.

Because that's my reality and it can readily become yours.

I've coached thousands of men and women to become self-made and to earn hundreds of thousands and even millions of dollars per year by expanding what they viewed as attainable and then sharing with them the most effective ways to create that reality as easefully as possible. I'm going to break it down for you, step by step, and share my story with you as we go. My hope is to inspire you that no matter how hard this path has been for you, or how much clarity you've lacked, or how unfair life has been to you up until now, that these three words ring loudly:

Up until now.

Up until now, you may have not known what to do or you may have had inconsistent income months or you may have felt like an impostor. You may have grossly undercharged for your services, stayed in a dead-end job, or made poor financial decisions. Up until now.

Draw a line in the sand with me. While your past or your upbringing and conditioning certainly are among the factors that influence what is possible or likely to happen for you in this life, they do not have the final say. You, my love, have the final say. You can opt into a new future that is independent of your past. If you saw the details of my past (and you'll see a lot of them here in this book), it appeared unlikely that I'd ever be a multimillionaire living her dream life in Bali. For years I was single, shy, and scraping by. For years I lived in substandard housing, traveled alone until the corporate money ran out, and lacked clarity about my long-term future. I was having a great time, sometimes, but it felt shortsighted and was short-lived during those years.

I didn't see myself as an entrepreneur. Yet here I am. An unlikely outcome that came from some hard, intentional pumping of the brakes, aggressive pivoting at some of the many forks in the road of life, purposeful tossing out of the old garbage weighing me down, and gleefully gunning it down the right side of the highway, all while figuring out exactly which exits I needed to take.

For your journey through this book, I'll tell you what I tell all my students and high-level mastermind clients: Take what resonates and leave the rest. You don't have to use all the strategies in this book to see huge improvements in your life and business. Applying the ones that resonate with you consistently over time, with intention, will drastically move the needle.

You're here for a few golden nuggets, in fact. There are a lot of words in this book, but only a tiny handful of them are what you came for. You've come for a sentence or two. One story that makes you remember yourself. One example of my clients that speaks to you and awakens something in you. You're here for one lead-generation strategy that brings in a tidal wave of new interest. You're here to birth one simple offer that becomes the bedrock of your business for the next five years. You're here for one idea, one inspiration, one nudge that goes on to help you make millions.

While you're here, don't be a stranger. I love hearing from my students as they take my digital courses, and I'd love to hear from you, dear reader, as you go through the book. Tag me on Instagram (@heyelainaray) and share a photo of an excerpt of the book that's speaking to you. Drop me a message and tell me what you've loved and what awakened in you through reading my story. You can also find dozens of resources on my website, www.elainaray.com, to help you grow your business in more depth than we can possibly cover in these pages. You'll find free trainings, masterclasses, self-study courses, and even masterminds and private coaching opportunities at a huge variety of price points to help you at whatever stage of the journey you're currently experiencing.

As we get started here, I want you to know that you are powerful beyond measure. And you can get unlikely, unrealistic results very quickly.

> OPEN YOURSELF UP RIGHT NOW TO PLEASANT SURPRISES, QUANTUM LEAPS, AND UNLIKELY OUTCOMES MANIFESTING WITH GREAT SPEED AND EASE. DECIDE TO BE WILLING TO SEE THINGS DIFFERENTLY THAN YOU HAVE UP UNTIL NOW AND TO MUSTER UP A NEW LEVEL OF COURAGE TO STEP INTO A VERSION OF YOURSELF YOU'VE ALWAYS SUPPOSED WAS INSIDE OF YOU AND WHO IS NOW READY TO TAKE THE REINS.

There are no rules. You can come out of the gate swinging. You hold the vision and set the standards. You can show up as the new kid on the block in your niche or industry and turn heads. You can make $100 this month and $10,000 the next. You can launch one right offer and go from five clients to fifty. You can write one post and attract three hundred leads. I've seen my clients do all the above firsthand, with simple moves and lots of backing those moves like the force of nature they are.

Your influence and compensation do not have to incrementally increase in a practical and likely fashion so as to not startle or intimidate someone. Realistically, if you take the words of this book to heart, your work is going to explode. You will cause a disruption in your segment of the market by doing the things outlined in the lessons portion of each chapter, doing the assignments, and taking immediate action. And you'll probably spin your own head trying to catch up with who you are becoming along the way. The identity shifts and DNA upgrades will take place at the speed of *destiny*.

Read this book with an open heart and mind. Open yourself up right now to pleasant surprises, quantum leaps, and unlikely outcomes manifesting with great speed and ease. Decide to be willing to see things differently than you have up until now and to muster up a new level of courage to step into a version of yourself you've always supposed was inside of you and who is now ready to take the reins.

This work can set you free. Choose to cast off the ties to the old operating system you've been running and embark on the greatest healing and personal growth journey of your life: becoming self-made.

CHAPTER 1

HONORING YOUR SOUL-KNOWING AND LISTENING FOR NUDGES (OR SHOVES) IN THE RIGHT DIRECTION

TAURANGA, NEW ZEALAND
JUNE 9, 2017

I'll never forget the feeling in my stomach when I opened my laptop on a Friday morning and my corporate email displayed an unusual error message.

I was working out of a literal motel in a remote town on the north island of New Zealand. A small crew of Kiwi Uber drivers and I were isolated on the windy coast while mapping every street of cities across the country in the name of a future with self-driving cars.

It was my third country in nine months. My previous placements in Mexico and Australia trained me to be a "city launcher," a seemingly glamorous job working for one of the world's most booming companies at the time.

When I applied for the position as a contractor for Uber's international projects arm, I had just washed up on the shores of San Francisco after eighteen months backpacking alone through the world, starting with a stint in my would-be future home of Bali and winding my way through all of Southeast Asia, Burma, Nepal, India (where I disappeared into the best parts of myself for about four months), and Europe. Naturally, in the due course of any quarter-life hippie wanderings, I finally landed at Burning Man for the first time.

By the time the man burned, my money from the last round of corporate brown nosing and ladder climbing had run out. I was officially sleeping on the couches of some new Burning Man campmates in the Mission District, and I knew it was time to go back to having a paycheck.

Despite my precarious financial situation and insatiable wanderlust, I had a safe, shiny résumé with IBM management consulting experience, near native Spanish and Chinese speaking skills from college, and the necessary lack of attachments to easily qualify for international program manager positions whenever I tired of living the backpacker's dream, which was roughly every two years back in those days.

I landed the job as a contractor for Uber and was sent to Mexico City for training, back on the breast and getting direct deposits to my checking account every two weeks.

However, the shiniest résumé in the world couldn't overcome the fact that, at the soul level, I didn't want to be in meetings, even in trendy start-up offices in Sydney or Mexico City—I wanted to be back on the banks of the Ganges River in northern India, sitting at the feet of my yoga guru, and feeling the wind in my hair while driving a motorbike through the mountains of Burma.

It shouldn't have come as a surprise when nine months later, I opened my personal email inbox from a three-star motel in small town New Zealand and saw the email that made my stomach drop and my heart flip in my chest:

Subject: Termination of Contract

I was fired.

The email (not even a phone call, how nice is that?) specified that I was to immediately pack up my belongings, head to the airport, and be on the next flight home to make room for my replacement. I was being fired for "performance issues" and "poor judgment and leadership," and there was only the slightest hint of diplomatic niceties as I was being booted to the doorstep of the rest of my life.

I felt like a colossal failure.

In my previous jobs, I was always the top performer. As a management consultant at IBM, I was the top pick by the partners for projects. I was the one coordinating global mentorship initiatives, social gatherings for the entire New York City office, and volunteering my time in other departments to expand my skill set beyond consulting. As a director for another employer I had in Europe, I crushed sales targets, met presidents of countries, and signed six-figure contracts with the likes of the International Development Bank . . . in Spanish *and* English.

I had never failed.
I had never dreamed of being fired.

But I had never woken up, seen the world, or had my heart blasted open the way I did during that last trek around the planet. I was a different human now, and an unemployable one, it seemed.

I had been initiated onto ancient paths of yoga and meditation in India.

I had a spiritual awakening that invited me to quit drinking alcohol and eating meat.

I had trekked ten days solo through the Nepalese Himalayas, completely alone in the vast silence of nature, fighting altitude sickness on one of the highest passes in Asia.

I had hitchhiked through Burma, utterly flinging myself into the most chaotic, adventurous parts of the world where I wouldn't see anyone else like me for weeks at a time. (I once ventured so far north into unheard of parts of Burma that I was apprehended by officials and forced to fly back to Yangon for my own safety. I liked traveling and living on the edge.)

I met travelers who had been on the road for two to three *years,* making stops on every continent and slowly savoring all the flavors of the world.

I had met expats living in Bali, Berlin, and Thailand, free to make their own schedules and work from their laptops in cafés in the jungle.

These imprints forever changed the course of my life. I couldn't know that so much freedom was possible, then go back to the confines of an office where I'd help a billion-dollar company make another billion dollars.

But I also didn't see myself as an entrepreneur. The idea intimidated me, and I couldn't identify with it.

Now back to Tarangua.

Fired.

I was a woman who had just been thrown overboard by the illusion of safety of the last J-O-B I would ever have. I needed a life raft. Could I perhaps become a *freelancer*? Entrepreneur, business owner, millionaire . . . these words were not yet part of my vocabulary.

Blinking at the email with angry tears welling up in my eyes, I had to fly myself "home" to a home I didn't have. I had left the US four years prior (more on that story later). All my belongings were split between the two suitcases I carried with me and what was in boxes in my parents' basement in Buffalo, New York, much to their dismay.

I stormed out of the motel, grabbed the keys to the rental car, and with tires squealing in the faces of stunned colleagues who were probably thinking that the girl who just got fired shouldn't be taking off with the company car, I went to make the hardest phone call of my life.

Standing with my toes in the sand on a beach near Mount Maunganui, 8,590 miles from where I was born, I called my parents, heartbroken, with my tail between my legs.

I gave them the surreal news that I, Elaina Giolando, lifetime high achiever, had been fired.

And worse than that, I needed a place to live while I put together a new life plan.

My parents took the news well and were extremely supportive while I cried bitterly alone on the other side of the world. They told me I had two weeks of free room and board back in Buffalo before I had to get it together.

Deal.

They were exhausted by my reckless international adventures and bottomless one-way ticket purchases to places like Bolivia, Egypt, South Africa, and Mongolia, but I wasn't.

After I hung up the phone and cried my pitiful tears stemming from feeling like a total failure, I felt a profound shift I'll never forget.

As I walked along the shoreline picking up dozens of seashells, the faintest hints of possibility seemed to open up to me.

I thought about my dad, a lifelong construction worker who spent the last three decades working on a roof installing heating and air conditioning units in both the bitter winter cold and the sticky upstate summer heat.

Maybe I could help him start a company where he could do "side jobs" for households and small companies and free him from the 5 a.m. start times he'd kept up since I was a little girl watching him get into his work van and run the engine so the windows could defrost while he filled up his coffee mug.

It seemed like such a hard life; I'd noticed it even as a kid.

As a recently fired/freed-up twenty-seven-year-old, I felt the reckoning of my father's perhaps unmet dreams and desires stir in my gut.

I didn't want to repeat history.

I picked up more seashells and more ideas came.

My blog, Life Before 30, could be turned into more of a moneymaker. I occasionally coached clients who came through organic Google traffic and found my travel writings or saw my column on Fortune.com about unconventional careers. I'd faithfully written blogs almost every night while I worked my nine-to-five for more than five years, and now, without a full-time job, I would have time to hone my craft and find a way to monetize my precious blog.

I felt scared as I walked the beach, but full of hope. I felt the awakening of the part of me that was an "ideas" person. A fighter. A woman determined to be financially autonomous.

When the plane landed twenty-seven hours later at Buffalo Niagara International Airport and my parents greeted me, I gifted them a huge jar of seashells from the other side of the world, each one a reminder of the moments that marked my transition from the world of dependence on someone else for my survival to the world where I would move freely with my time, money, energy, and unconfined brilliance.

They were a reminder of the day the rug was ripped out from underneath me, where my soul spoke for me and said *NO. We will go no further along this deviated path.*

The day when I was kicked out of the house by the universe and ungraciously shoved in a new direction.

Sometimes you're not brave enough to do the thing your soul desires most, but it will happen for you anyway—most likely in an abrupt, jarring, and unplanned sort of way that is ultimately in your highest good.

Little did I know that just four years after that heart-wrenching day, I would become a millionaire of my very own company doing what I love while living on a paradisiacal tropical island. That I would be helping thousands of men and women follow their true calling and monetize their gifts.

The start-up bros in San Francisco who fired me? Thank you. Without you, I would still be working for a few thousand dollars per month, deeply unfulfilled, and stalling on my buried dream to be a leader of something bigger than myself.

You were my angels.

If you are moving through a void in your own life right now (perhaps you've recently left a job, gotten fired, had a previous business fail, went through a breakup, or started a new venture or entered a big new chapter of an existing venture that feels uncertain), know this: The void is your friend. The void is unavoidable.

> IT'S UNFOLDING IN YOUR FAVOR. ALWAYS. TRUST IT.

When you're destined for a different kind of life, when you're meant to have more of an impact, when you're choosing something that most people don't dare to choose, you will have to pass through many moments when there is a high degree of uncertainty at play by choice or by force.

Your job is to get comfortable in the abyss. In these moments, you get to learn to trust something deeper and bigger than you and know that when you are here to touch others, the whole tapestry of life becomes much more interwoven and tangible in how it touches your life in turn. Unseen and unfelt support is there for you. Guidance is all around you in the form of your angels (the people in your life), in any kind of universal and ethereal support you believe in and work with (the other kind of angels), and in the form of decisions that are made for you by doors closing and opportunities vanishing in order to powerfully and properly redirect you.

Your job is to trust this guidance and know that in the moments of taking a big leap or in times of great uncertainty that you are being guided by your future self. A higher knowing and greater intelligence is working with you, through you, and for you.

It's unfolding in your favor. Always. Trust it.

These are the words I wish someone would have told me when I was sitting on that plane returning to Buffalo, banished and ashamed and scared. These are the words, perhaps not as developed and wise as they are now, that I slowly formed over time through my own process of self-reflection in the months and years that followed.

And it's okay to grieve a big shift that is unintended or surprising to you. Looking back now, I didn't grieve the cutting of my cords to the corporate world and the slam of the door in my face. I probably carried trauma and shock from that event in my body for a lot longer than necessary because I didn't realize at the time how important it was to mourn that loss. Even though better things were coming for me, and I have zero regrets about how things ended at Uber, I would have moved on sooner had I taken time to be with the pain, rejection, and loss of that job and that whole part of my life.

It's like coming out of a relationship. The more you're able to hold yourself in the sadness and loneliness during your transition, the more healing becomes available to you, leaving you open for an even more aligned relationship because you chose growth and conscious grieving.

Any major shift in identity, even for the ultimate betterment and service of your life path, can be marked by two sides: *what you look forward to embracing* and *what you must let go of in order to embrace it.*

How many engaged women grieve the loss of their singlehood? Not because they aren't happy about getting married but because they are aware of letting go of one sense of freedom and one chapter of their life.

How many women grieve becoming mothers? Not because they aren't excited about becoming a mom but because simultaneously they are losing life as they knew it beforehand. A chapter closes.

I bet not many.

In my story, even though I was truly aligned to leave the corporate world and, on a soul level, was tremendously relieved and trusting in my new path, I still would have benefited from conscious grieving the transition itself, especially considering how badly and how suddenly it shattered my reality from one moment to the next.

I also wished that I had exercised more faith and trust in the process of transition from the get-go because (as you'll see in the chapters to come) my healing journey and figuring out how to "make it" outside the confines of the nine-to-five world took me some years, trials, and tribulations to piece together. Had I known that it's completely safe to be redirected in life, and sometimes the most painful thing is exactly what you needed all along, I would have found my path even sooner.

You have the opportunity now to a) listen to the whispers of your soul's calling before they turn into a rude awakening by being more in tune with your truth and intuition, b) when change does occur, whether or not you want it to, get on board as fast as possible with the energy of trust and faith in what's unfolding being for your highest good, and c) be conscious of any grieving and letting go that needs to happen as you go through fast evolution and rapid identity shifts that could potentially leave skid marks on your heart.

HOMEWORK FOR THIS CHAPTER

1. Where is there a whisper of guidance right now that already knows the next step? Where are you honoring that voice and where may you be in danger of ignoring it?

2. What transition(s) in your life, past or present, do you need to grieve or do additional processing work around? Set a time and space to do that intentionally. Trust yourself to be guided to do it in a way that is perfect and meaningful for you.

3. Think back to a time when you were clearly redirected by a force greater than you. What do you know now about why that had to happen that you couldn't have known then? How has it made you better and wiser?

4. How can you choose to tap into more faith and trust that everything is unfolding for your greater good and supporting you in your life right now?

5. Where is there a void in your life or business right now that is challenging you and that you get to choose to accept? What growth do you imagine is waiting for you on the other side?

6. Picture yourself twelve months from now on the other side of the big uplevel you're currently in, completely happy and in peace. Tell the story to your current self about how you got there. What needed to happen along the way for the eventual results to come?

CHAPTER 2

DROPSHIPPING T-SHIRTS OR DOING MY SOUL WORK?

LAKE MALAWI, SOUTHEAST AFRICA
OCTOBER 3, 2017

I paced around the shoreline. I often seem to go to the water for answers, and this time I was trying to get cell reception as sweat poured from my armpits and down the backs of my knees, while a group of local kids eyeballed me from the fishing boats that floated a few meters away.

On the other end of the line was a guy in Miami who was making $20,000+ per month selling yoga pants made in China on Amazon with a concept called "dropshipping." He was trying to enroll me into his course, and I was lapping it up like a thirsty dog.

"Okay, I'm in," I told him and hung up resolutely, then headed to my literal grass hut to pull out my laptop and send him $1,500 with the hope of making a small fortune with his knowledge of the e-commerce market.

In all honesty, it was a desperate means to an end.

I told myself that if I could pull in even a few thousand dollars per month with a cleverly selected product, then I could focus full time on my blog and do what I really wanted to do: get paid to write.

Meanwhile, I was fulfilling a lifelong dream of spending time in a remote African village volunteering for a nonprofit organization.

In fact, I had just spent five hours squished in a local bus that smelled of petrol, dried fish, and bananas from a tiny village outside of Blantyre, Malawi, where I had lived with a family that made it their soul mission to get underaged kids (often orphans) who had been wrongfully imprisoned out of jail and back on their feet. It was amazing.

And after a month in the village and drinking water purified with bleach, eating only eggs, rice, and peanut butter, and being the only foreigner, no less a blonde woman, in the hottest month in what must be the hottest country in Africa, my dream felt complete.

I fundraised thousands of dollars for the organization, I left them with templated documents to attract continuous donors, and I got to see a part of the world I had always felt called to. (I had worked extensively in other parts of Africa as an expat for one of my former companies and spent more than a year between 2013 and 2015 living in places like Lagos, Nigeria, Johannesburg, South Africa, and Addis Ababa, Ethiopia, but I yearned to venture deep into the Heart of Africa, as Malawi is fondly called, and give back after my time in the cities.)

I was actively checking off items on my bucket list . . . and it felt wonderful.

***

So how did I get here—standing on the shores of Lake Malawi wire transferring a guy $1,500 to teach me about the most profitable rabbit holes of Amazon.com?

It started back when I spontaneously decided to set up shop in Berlin for the summer after my two-week grace period at my parents' nest in Buffalo expired, where by the grace of God I landed an online job as a freelance matchmaker for a start-up out of New York. I made $100 per date that my clients went on, and it was enough to live on while I figured out a better plan.

It was in Berlin where I met up with my best friend from college, danced in the underground techno clubs like Berghain, and visited the vibrant coworking spaces where I felt the pulse of a life that existed well outside of NYC office hours. While sipping lattes in Kreuzberg, I met start-up founders, bloggers, freelancers, journalists, e-commerce shop owners . . . and "dropshippers."

I still didn't identify with being an entrepreneur or even an aspiring entrepreneur. At this point, I just needed to eat, and I had vowed to never compile another résumé again.

The offbeat culture of Berlin and her renegade twenty-something population was all the fuel I needed to know that it was possible for me to make it without relying on a paycheck. I held the faith, used my tiny freelance income, and pursued my relentless desire to travel the world.

Berlin led me to that moment in Malawi, with my curiosity around dropshipping and alternative income streams percolating alongside my relentless pursuit of international adventure and a passion for nonprofit work. I was beginning to see a way to make this globe-trotting lifestyle—and what I loved about being able to pick up and fly one way to Africa at a moment's notice—sustainable.

After my time in Malawi, I was guided to study with my spiritual teachers back in India for a few months, once again appreciative for the total freedom to be pulled by my heartstrings to another continent. I studied tantra, meditation, and yoga in the foothills of the Himalayas, still making ends meet with my tiny blog and freelance-writing income. I continued to explore the world in this phase, moving to a farm in Hawaii and living in a literal Home Depot toolshed (living in Hawaii was on the bucket list . . . the toolshed was not) while handpicking papayas every morning, **before finally realizing it was time to get serious about figuring** out a stable income stream to support my very unstable but very heart-driven, travel-oriented lifestyle.

This deepening of my commitment to my passions and my true soul-knowing led me to the biggest move of my life up until that point: returning to Bali.

A whisper of intuition told me it was time to plant roots and seek out a like-minded community where I could be supported on this new life path.

I bought a one-way ticket to Bali, Indonesia, a place I had visited twice on my travels around the world, the ornate palatial walls of the homes in Ubud beckoning to me. Exactly one week later, a tragic volcanic eruption wiped out the entire region where I'd been living on the rugged **Big Island of Hawaii**, which included burying my toolshed in fifty feet of molten lava.

The whisper was not off base.

On my last visit to Bali in 2016 before my round-the-world adventure, I had promised myself that someday, when I had the means to support myself with nothing more than a laptop and an internet connection, I'd be back to mingle with the extraordinary community of people she summoned from all around the world. I, too, would live in a bungalow in the jungle and become friends with full-time entrepreneurs, freelancers, and artists who, like me, refused to go about things the easy, normal way.

And so it was.

It didn't take long for the whisper of Bali that saved me from the Hawaiian volcanic eruption to lead me to the exact wisdom I needed to navigate my new chapter.

I'll never forget telling my new friend Rusty about my dropshipping course months after that day pacing around Lake Malawi.

Up until that point, I had gone through the Miami guy's materials and put together several spreadsheets of potential products I could sell for a **few dollars of profit per sale: camping lights with USB chargers and chaga** mushroom powders that were up-and-coming herbal supplements were among my top choices that would amass me my fortune.

Rusty, a serial entrepreneur and real estate investor from Australia whom I deeply admired, looked at me sideways and pursed his lips before dropping his truth bomb on me.

It's like he could smell the deviated path I was going down, *again*, and he wasn't going to be an accomplice to it.

"What do you *really* want to do, Elaina? Sell camping lights or write your blog and help people?"

I blinked back at him. "Write. Coach more people in my sessions that I sell off my website. Definitely. I just don't know how, and I need something to help me make money so I can do that."

"You are the product, my friend. I see it in you. You were born for the limelight. You are your own brand. Invest in *you*. Invest in making that work."

That same day, I dropped dropshipping.

I got clear on how much I actually wanted to make it my job to learn, write, teach, inspire, and help people.

I had found, and remembered, my calling.

ESSENTIALLY, SEE WHO YOU'RE MEANT TO BE AND DECIDE TO BE THAT PERSON NOW.

The biggest lesson I can offer you here, my dear reader, is to beware of doing things as a means to the end when you're starting to get the sense of your heart's big desire and direction.

Beware of thinking that you need to do

something to make money first *so then* you can start your own clothing line. That you need to get a bunch of certifications and get someone else's stamp of approval before you're able to share your wisdom and create a business around your own valuable life experience. That you need to make a certain amount of money before you hire a coach or get support from a team member. That you need to make more money so you have time to write your book.

Start the clothing line using a loan if you need to. Share your experiences and design offers to help people with the same problems you've overcome. Hire the coach or team member you feel called to hire. Make time to write your book. Do the thing now, without unnecessary story and conditions around it. If you've thought of it, it's for a reason. It's safe guidance, and it's already yours.

Essentially, see who you're meant to be and decide to be that person now. Any form of "I need to do *this* so then I can do *that*" when you really just want to be doing *that* is a big fat trap. Do the thing you know you're meant to be doing as soon and as loudly and as confidently as you can as soon as you know. You'll never feel ready, you'll never get permission, you'll never have all the resources, you'll never see all the steps before you take the first one, you'll never know how, you've just got to know that what you've noticed inside of you is real, and it's meant for you, and you can have it without delay or detour to other stops on the journey you don't really want to make. Those are not aligned actions or places for you if you don't deeply desire them for their sake only.

And you *already know* what's right for you and what's not. You know what it is you're meant to be doing. The only thing that's possibly getting in the way if you have any degree of uncertainty around it right now is conditioning that's telling you a story about why you can't have, be, or do the thing you've always sensed in your bones is the thing for you. Try to identify the story that's clouding your vision and then look behind it. That's the thing. It's always been the thing for you.

Listen to the tiny pulls and tugs of intuition. Notice the moments throughout your day where you come alive. The wisdom and knowing is within you, and it's been with you since before you were born. It is safe to trust it, and it's safe to take risks, make big leaps, move before you're ready, and claim the future vision of yourself you know is possible for you. Do not delay.

HOMEWORK FOR THIS CHAPTER

1. Keep a running list of where and when you feel most alive throughout your day. What are you doing? Who are you with? What's the sensation that turns you on? Where do you lose your sense of time because you're so absorbed in the joy of the moment?

2. What is the thing that it's always been about for you? Close your eyes and travel a few years into the future and speak to the version of you who has everything you want, who is happy and successful and at ease. Ask that version of you what he or she is doing. Ask how he or she got there. Ask for clues about what you need to know and do now to get there, too.

3. Make a list of every tiny thing you do during your day in your work and personal life. Take a red pen and circle everything you're doing as a means to an end, not because it's really what you want to be doing now. Delegate or terminate these actions in your life. If you're not able to do either of those, find a way to shift the energy behind this action so you can get behind it and feel better about it and then set a timeline for getting it out of your life altogether.

4. Where do you doubt your ability to be an entrepreneur or be as successful as you desire to be? List out every crazy story and then decide what truth you're going to choose instead. For example, "I don't have the network needed to find investors or clients" becomes "I am choosing to expand my network and meet new people all the time" and "the people I meet desire to collaborate and work with me on the projects that excite me." Write a new story.

5. What are the tiniest, softest, most subtle voices inside of you saying right now? Where are you being delivered wise and safe guidance from within you right now? What would you do differently effective immediately if you simply trusted this part of you?

CHAPTER 3

MY FIRST $100,000 IDEA

UBUD, BALI, INDONESIA
DECEMBER 14, 2018

I'll never forget the month I barely left my house, ensnared by the first idea that seemed to hold the real possibility of filling up my bank account and never having to work for someone else ever again.

I'll never forget the Christmas that came and went and not flying home to Mom and Dad because I couldn't afford the plane ticket from Indonesia to Buffalo. The sound of my last remaining dollars trickling out of my bank account was like the deafening roar of Niagara Falls to me.

Eighteen months after being rudely booted out of the last job I ever hoped to have, I was teetering on the edge of, well, the rest of my life.

My desperate balancing act had become exhausting, and I knew I was meant to do more than just survive as a freelancer making a few hundred dollars here and there to make rent in a foreign country with a low cost of living.

My attachment to struggle and survival became obvious to me.

And I was ready to change my tune.

I missed my comfortable salary. I missed booking flights on a corporate card and staying in the best hotels in the world. To think I had mingled with presidents and prime ministers of countries like Paraguay, Mongolia, and Guyana before becoming a wandering, jobless nomad. I had worked on Wall Street, for God's sake, and I'd proudly and pleasurably worn suits and heels.

I missed that side of myself.

Since moving to Bali, I'd spent nine months driving my scooter through the wide iridescent rice fields, hair blowing in the wind. I'd been enchanted by the constant smell of incense in the air, the temple music, and the dazzling volcanic scenery everywhere I'd turned my blonde head.

I'd definitely had one extended *Eat Pray Love* moment. After five years of various forms of ladder climbing and experiencing fast-paced city environments around the world, it was really nourishing.

During those months, I went to cacao ceremonies held under the moonlight where hundreds of people linked arms around a fire and chanted "Jaya!" while dancing barefoot on the grass. I went to yoga classes, became a yoga teacher for a short stint, learned to talk more about my feelings through things like "authentic relating" seminars, and sat Indian-style on the floor in vegan cafés while meeting the eclectic variety of Ubudians, some of whom felt like they had gotten rather stuck like a fly in a thick bowl of soup while circulating around this part of the world.

Just as I was awakening out of my own soupiness and feeling a desire to rejoin the rest of the world, I met Scott.

Scott was incredibly well informed about something I had no real idea about and rarely heard anyone else in my little corner of Bali talk about up until that point: internet marketing.

Scott taught me about funnels.

He taught me about lead magnets, $7 trip wires, and $97 courses that could lead to a small fortune. (Consult your nearest bro marketing manual for a translation.)

He made me realize that if I came up with my own $97 course and sold it to just 1,001 people, I would have $100,000, and I would be FREE!

Now I had a mission. I quit the cafés and cacao and got down to work.

Over that lonely Christmas and into the new year, I spent most of my days sitting on a rickety wooden chair positioned jussstttt so in front of the door to my bungalow talking to my iPhone. There were virtually no lights in the house, and I didn't have a professional camera set up with a boom mic and ring light. There was no money for those back then. I had a "Made in China" tripod balanced on a wooden box in front of me and about five hours of direct sunlight in the direction of my chair per day.

I had come up with an idea for my first course, which I called "Escape the Matrix." I spent weeks pouring over the outline, writing out my talking points, and taking hours per day to get one good take of each section. I painstakingly edited the videos myself in iMovie.

(Keep in mind that I now make $100,000 on a course launch before I even sit down to deliver the first module, and I teach my clients to do the same. We'll cover this in more detail later.)

Seeing myself on video was the first big challenge of my online career.

I had been a blog writer up until this point. I had written for *Fortune*, *Business Insider*, and *Fast Company*, but I absolutely buried myself behind my knack for the written word.

I felt cringeworthy teaching on camera. I thought I looked like a troll, and don't even get me started on how much I hated the sound of my own voice.

However, I decided it was an opportunity to practice the self-love these Ubudians talked about and got on with it, knowing my message was going to help a lot of people who couldn't even imagine leaving their job, traveling the world (alone! as a woman!) for five years, and moving to Bali to start their own business like I was doing.

I was brave.

I knew how to take risks.

I had an appetite for adventure the rest of the world should definitely be taking notes about.

My story mattered, that much I knew, and I knew there were thousands of people a few steps behind me who would benefit from the tools and tips I picked up along my journey around the world (a few times over).

After the arduous thirty days of filming and preparing and befriending myself on video, I was ready to launch.

Scott, bless his heart and patience, helped me understand ClickFunnels.

I made my first email list.

I made my first funnel.

I got my hands dirty.

And dare I say, I loved it.

The day I pressed Publish on Escape the Matrix, first original course by Elaina Giolando, I was over the moon.

I shared a post on Facebook about it, published a blog inviting people to buy it, and put a button front and center on my website at the time, Life Before 30.

Anticipation kept me awake at night. I kept refreshing my ClickFunnels page to see how many page views and sales came in, convinced I would soon be flooded with thousands of dollars, allowing my struggle chapter to firmly close. I had worked so hard for this moment.

The days went by . . .

Which turned into weeks . . .

And I sold exactly two courses.

$194 minus taxes.

Little did I know that one of those sales would eventually turn into a multi-thousand-dollar coaching client, among my first "premium" sales, from a man who would become a lifelong friend and ally in the industry. Truly, in that moment, an empire was born.

But in January 2019, after a long winter's work in my moldy cave balancing my tripod in front of a simple wooden chair, I felt like a failure.

NO ONE JUST WALKS UP TO THE ONLINE WORLD AND DROPS THEIR FIRST OFFER AND MAKES ONE HUNDRED GRAND. NO ONE KNOWS HOW TO DO IT UNTIL THEY'VE DONE IT.

Take it from present-day me who launches a course and does $50,000, $100,000, even $200,000 in sales from it, no one who has the results you want now started out getting these results. No one just walks up to the online world and drops their first offer and makes one hundred grand. No one knows how to do it until they've done it. *Read that again.* You're going in blind, my friend. Naturally, it's 1,000 percent better if you have a coach or mentor by your side to show you a few things they've learned along the way, but even then, it's going to still fundamentally be trial and error when you start out doing something you've never done before. There's no way around it except to create space for it.

What I want to tell you now is to embrace the process. Embrace the flopped launches, the products that fail, the ideas you thought were so good that only make you $194. It's all part of the process, and as long as you keep going and keep getting support, you'll one day be writing the story of your first flop in your book, and it will be no big deal because you simply kept going. You launched it again. You made it better. You learned a lot. You *started.*

It's also good to remember at this stage that truly every step counts. Every sales call, every post, every course you invest in, every livestream you do, every website you make, every email you send, every little bit adds up and is all worthwhile.

The internet marketing tools I learned with my friend Scott back then were not appropriate for the stage of business I was in at the time, but I didn't know that then. I learned a few things out of order, and that's okay. It all served me in the long run because the funnels and digital courses and automation strategies I learned back then very much serve my business today and are utilized on a day-to-day basis. You never know when something you learn now is going to fit into the puzzle, so keep adding to your tool belt.

Case in point: As hard as it was getting on camera for the first time and teaching, and as much as those particular videos never really saw the light of day, doing it was still a huge milestone in my business. I've since made over two million dollars by doing a lot of my marketing on video, and this is how it all started, quite imperfectly.

On a strategic note, one thing I can say to save you some of the pain of my failed course launch is to teach you how to do it properly. In a nutshell, sell the course before you create it. Come up with an idea, do your market research and test that it's something people you want to serve want to learn from you (I teach this in detail inside my famous *Signature Offers That Sell* course), and then create a sales page. Tell them what they are going to learn inside and generally how it's structured and what will be included. You don't have to have every module completely mapped out before you deliver it. Most of the time when I create a new course, I don't even know all the modules we'll cover, and if they are listed on the sales page, it's a rough estimate and likely to change. The most important aspect is that the overall outcome the client is going to get is solid—you know the main steps and things they'll learn to get there and what they'll walk away with. That's more than enough to put it out there and sell it.

Then, if (and only if!) people buy it, you create it, and you create it by delivering the teachings live. Do not sit in your living room and record and rerecord the thing to perfection. You do not need to film it in HD or hire a team to edit the recordings. It's the transformation that occurs from someone being exposed to the material and the way *you* embody the result that helps your students get their own results. Before a session, have some notes ready, teach in a natural and engaging way to the people who join live, then save the recording. You can even do live Q&As and get direct feedback from the people taking the course as you go, so you'll naturally fill in any gaps in the curriculum you wouldn't have thought of sitting in your living room alone that you get from having the right person with the right problem in front of you as you teach.

Finally, after you deliver the course live and have been paid to create it, you can then sell it as a digital product (a.k.a. a self-study course) through a funnel, or live launch it again but with the material already complete. You can then move on to the next topic and course and keep expanding your body of work. This method keeps your creativity flowing and leads to generating more signature teachings. Eventually, you can hire an expert to build email automations and funnels that generate passive income from all your existing courses. If one particular course idea doesn't sell, do more market research and launch it again, or run with a new idea. Keep going and keep adding to your body of work.

HOMEWORK FOR THIS CHAPTER

1. List twenty-five different ways you could make $100,000 just as a thought exercise to get your creative juices flowing. Circle your top five and then pick one to get started on today.

2. What is one idea you have been holding on to that you can produce quickly and launch in the next thirty days or less?

3. What is the biggest failure you've had to date in your business and how is it unexpectedly serving and supporting you today?

4. Scott was my angel in this chapter. Who is your angel? Write down at least ten names of people you can connect with to help you learn something new, improve your business, or collaborate with in some way. Reach out to three of them right now.

5. If you had to launch a digital course on some aspect of your expertise or life experience in the next thirty days, what would it be about? What's stopping you from putting it out there? Can you choose to put those stories aside and do it anyway?

CHAPTER 4

THE BREAKDOWN BEFORE THE BREAKTHROUGH: MY HEALING JOURNEY

BALI, INDONESIA
ANAND ASHRAM
JANUARY 22, 2019

I'll never forget the evening I gunned my scooter down a remote country road outside of Ubud, the wide rice terraces swirling past me at sunset. Sparks of sunlight glimmered over the green oceans of scalloped land and tears streamed down my face as I drove.

I had seemingly arrived at the end point of an eighteen-month journey to make it on my own as an entrepreneur.

Mastering a one-handed throttle, I nudged tears off my face with my fingers and squinted at the potholed road in front of me, alternating between chanting Hindu mantras to Ganesha and praying to my childhood Christian God.

It must have not been an entirely uncommon scene on an island where millions of people from all over the world come for healing (sometimes I do wonder what the Balinese think of the foreigners who come to Bali to learn obscure emotional healing processes and make wild sounds in the night doing ayahuasca), but I felt ridiculously messy and moderately insane speaking things out into the wind like:

"Why is this so hard for me?"

"I don't know how much longer I can struggle and be lost."
"My money is running out. I don't know what to do now."
"I need help. I see who I'm meant to be, but I just can't seem to get there. Please guide me."
"I can't go back. Please don't make me go back."

Dressed in all white, I was heading to an *Agnihotri* (fire) ceremony at an ashram I had heard about. After my three months living in an ashram in India with my teacher Yogrishi Vishvektu back in 2018, I was searching for the same traditional path of yoga I had found on the banks of the Ganges, and I had found it back home in Bali.

In many instances, we're simply pulled to things, guided in certain directions, and led to the experiences we're meant to have. This was one of them for me.

I felt guided to be at the ceremony that night, a type of ceremony I've done hundreds of times, multiple times per day with my teachers in India—symbolic of healing, transformation, and letting go.

As soon as I arrived at the ashram, blurry eyed and with smudged mascara, I was given a tour from one of the local guides with a hushed voice who briefly showed me the various shrines, then invited me to do a cleansing process by washing my feet and head before heading to the large group of Balinese and a few foreigners who were already singing, chanting, and praying before the fire ceremony started.

One shrine was inside a cave with a huge ornate Ganesha statue. A Balinese devotee sat in front, meditating and chanting an intoxicating mantra. I was immediately hooked into the same feeling I used to get when stepping out of 5 a.m. meditation in Rishikesh and standing on the rooftop of the ashram in utter bliss, bathing in the first specks of daylight piercing through the foothills of the Himalayas, yanking me into spiritual ecstasy.

I've always had a bit of monk energy in me. My whole business was created to ultimately support me to live this kind of life, dancing between my no-nonsense, get-shit-done, build-a-multimillion-dollar-company mentality and being deep in a familiar spiritual practice that involves not removal from the world but immersion into it from a state of devotion and higher consciousness.

In my travels, I had fallen in love with the temples of Nepal, Vipassana meditation in India, Balinese ceremonies, and quiet ashram life as much as I had the nightlife of Tokyo and Lagos in other stages of my journey.

Reminded of one of my deepest soul longings, I abandoned the guide, **plopped down in front of the magnificent statue, and continued the** prayer I had begun on my scooter earlier that evening.

I chanted the Ganesha mantra, calling on the sounds and syllables that millions of devotees have used for thousands of years for support and resilience in their lives. I cried quietly, not wanting to cause a scene. But I cried deeply.

It felt like the end of the road for me.

I had reached a moment when I'd either accept that I couldn't have exactly what I had desired and resign myself to not being able to use my time and energy in my lifetime in the way that my heart longed for . . .

. . . or there'd be a miraculous intervention.

Eventually I left, dried my tears, joined the ceremony, and forgot about my prayer after that night.

But something very interesting emerged in the days and weeks to follow. Something unexpected.

I started to notice tension and pain in my back.

I started to remember that I had a gnarly curve in my spine. My yoga teachers at the ashram noticed it, and I became aware of the fact that I had scoliosis for the first time at age twenty-eight. I don't remember having it as a child, so to this day it's hard to say when and how it emerged.

But I suddenly started to feel the call to get help with it. It felt important.

A series of nudges, awakening intuition, and curiosity led me to the living room of a British healer, bodyworker, and osteopath in Ubud who changed the course of my life.

When I told him I wanted to get an adjustment to correct the curvature of my spine, he said, "That's like saying to me, 'I found a streetlight in Hong Kong.' We've got a whole city and universe of problems to look at here."

What began to unfold and become clear was that I had a lifetime of grief, contraction, and emotional stagnation that had collected in my muscular tissue and was causing, on a psychosomatic level, the scoliosis.

It's a part of my story I haven't often told, mostly because it sounds crazy to most people.

The emotional congestion in my spine was, however, directly correlated to my stagnation as an aspiring entrepreneur.

Staying in a pattern of life where I wasn't living my truth, struggling with money and purpose and self-worth, and going in and out of the corporate world hoping to arrive where I wanted to be "someday" put me in a severely contracted state.

I needed to heal before I could lead the way I knew I was meant to lead.

The contraction in my body mirrored the contraction in my world.

Over my first few sessions, I had explosions of tears or fits of rage that would start in the osteopathic sessions while he worked on the musculature of my spine and end after days of me crying and grieving in bed in my villa.

I had tapped into a seemingly bottomless pit of grief through my spine.

The physical transformation was palpable and mind blowing. Within a few months, my spine had straightened considerably, largely from the effects of huge emotional releases of unknown origin. It eventually straightened completely, and my curve is almost imperceptible today.

I didn't need to know cognitively what caused the emotional releases or what it was all about. The fact was that grief, rage, and fear were held deeply in my psyche and in my body, and they needed to be felt. After six long yet fast-paced years of constant travel and corporate achievement, I needed to slow down (or rather come to a screeching, attention-getting halt) for it to bubble up and be acknowledged, seen, and moved.

I continued to see this wonderful healer for more than two years. At the beginning, I invested hundreds of dollars per session for multiple sessions per month, month after month. It was money I didn't feel I "should" be spending, and it hurt to miss it, but I knew the sessions were removing deep-seated blockages to my success.

And they were.

Because merely weeks into my initial treatment, I made another huge life-changing decision: I decided to end the part of this journey where I was going it alone and hire my first coach (more on that to come).

What I want you to see here is this: Leadership isn't about the glamorous moments or the entrepreneurial highlight reel. It's about the work that goes into the leader behind closed doors—and there's immense value in the inner game.

Leadership is about how we show up when we've hit a roadblock, who we decide to become when it doesn't look like what we want is going to happen, and how we treat ourselves and each other. The softer moments and times of reflection, personal challenge, and emotional healing add up. They become our internal anchors that hold us steady no matter how much the elements try to weather and wear us or our business down. These are the things that ultimately lead most entrepreneurs to massive expansion: in their true ability to hold other people in their transformation, to lead a team, to wield more financial power, and to be more influential because, through healing, they've become safer and more aligned channels of their craft.

This is the real behind-the-scenes of the kind of work that will shape you as a person and evolve your soul as you get ready to step up even bigger on your mission.

> FOR ME, BUSINESS HAS ALWAYS BEEN THE VEHICLE FOR HEALING AND PERSONAL GROWTH WORK IN MY LIFE. IT'S NEVER BEEN ABOUT THE MONEY BUT ABOUT WHO I GET TO AND HAVE TO BECOME TO PLAY AT A LEVEL THAT REQUIRES LEADERSHIP, RESPONSIBILITY, EVOLUTION, AND VISIBILITY DIALED ALL THE WAY UP. LIKE YOU, I WANT TO LIVE A LIFE ON FULL VOLUME BACKED WITH MY FULL POTENTIAL.

For me, business has always been *the* vehicle for healing and personal growth work in my life. It's never been about the money but about who I get to and have to become to play at a level that requires leadership, responsibility, evolution, and visibility dialed all the way up. Like you, I want to live a life on full volume backed with my full potential.

The path of healing is required in order to be a leader. Full stop.

It requires miracles and many moments of asking for guidance and intervention when times are difficult. Whenever you think you can't go on or the way forward is blocked for you, know that you have a whole spiritual team of guides, ancestors, beings, and support just waiting for you to call on them. They are ready and willing to help should you choose to receive it, but you must open the door for that conversation. You have to opt in and come with an energy of humbleness and sincerity. The guidance and the nudges and the miracles will come. Just ask.

I also want to stress how much your physical well-being has everything to do with your success and sustainability as an entrepreneur. I know I couldn't do what I do today without my health. For this reason, I prioritize bodywork, therapy, energy work, and other modalities such as cleansing and detoxing, naturopathy, acupuncture, and proper diet and lifestyle choices to keep the vessel of my work, which is my body, as pristine and well taken care of as possible. Your body must be given the same care if you want to lead others, channel information, use your gifts, produce prolific creative work, and be in the highest degree of alignment and integrity with the message you're due to bring forth right now. It all adds up. It all matters.

And this part of the journey doesn't lend itself to mere incremental growth. Consistently investing in healing can provide explosive, nonsensical, illogical, wild, potent, and miraculous results. Sometimes it's a daily grind of going to one more therapy session, looking at one more hard thing from the past, healing one more part of your body that's been stiff and stuck. You can't predict the results that come from investing in yourself on the spiritual level, but what I do know is that in the long run, it's a quantum leap from where you'd be if you didn't intentionally support yourself this way.

Let it be said, finally, that it is not required that you feel complete or finished with your healing or your personal growth in order to be worthy as a thought leader, facilitator, or creator. This is an ongoing, never-ending process that is to be enjoyed and savored in and of itself. I'll be going to therapy until the day I die. I'll be investing in myself and discovering new things I get to learn about and improve upon until my last breath. That also does not mean that along the journey I won't simultaneously and paradoxically know that I am enough exactly as I am now. That I am loved. That I am worthy. That I am wise. That I have a lot to share and teach and that I have a message, although evolving, that matters enough to be shared today in its current state of evolution.

On a practical note, your community and audience love to witness your transformation. They love to come along for the ride. My audience has been with me online since 2011, and they've seen my journey unfold step by step. Let your people see you in the unfolding and allow them to be included in your process instead of presenting yourself as some shiny object that is completely done, finished, polished, and stale.

This is an industry where the more you embody the work and exemplify that you actively use the tools you teach, the better. Where you lead by example. Where your humanness has a very important seat at the table.

HOMEWORK FOR THIS CHAPTER

1. What are some other forms of support that might feel good to add to your life right now? Where is your curiosity leading you: therapy, energy work, life coaching, bodywork, cleansing, acupuncture, etc.? Choose one avenue and make a booking today to start exploring.

2. If you fully trusted that you had a team of guides and angels ready and willing to support you with anything you need, who had guidance ready at their fingertips to show to you, what would you ask for right now?

3. What is one way you can reveal more of your transformation and ongoing evolution with your audience and community, both in aspects that are relevant to your area of expertise in business and in areas of your personal life? Bring your people along on the ride with you.

4. What intuitive nudges are you receiving right now about parts of your body that might need your attention? How can you create more awareness and space to listen to your body?

5. What commitments around health, healing, and wellness are you willing to make right now for the next thirty days?

CHAPTER 5

THE DAY I MET MY FIRST COACH AND QUIT HOARDING MY ACORNS

UBUD, BALI, INDONESIA
MARCH 14, 2019

I distinctly remember that it was well over 100 degrees. The smell of spices, overripe bananas, and body odor from the other forty passengers on the bus from Lilongwe to Blantyre filled my nostrils. I was sandwiched between the window and a heavyset woman whose sputtering baby was uncomfortably close to my face. I spent the trip watching rural Malawi spin past me, vast stretches of flat nothingness dotted by small villages of huts and locals pedaling their bicycles on dusty dirt roads.

Every time the bus stopped to let a passenger off in the middle of nowhere of the African countryside, dozens of colorfully dressed women hawking dried fish, nuts, and more bananas would run to the side of the bus, yelling at every passenger to buy her goods. They were particularly entertained by the one pale face on the bus and would laugh uncontrollably at me, shoving the plastic bags of candies and fish through my window. Sweat gathered in wet patches behind my knees, under my sports bra, and most curiously, inside my ears. *Why did I do this again when there's a flight between the only two cities in this entire country?*

Well before I was an entrepreneur, I traveled on a shoestring budget around the world out of pure, reckless abandon into the wildness of the greatest possible adventure I could have. I wanted to be up close with the locals. I wanted to do the things they did. I wanted to step out of my skin and into theirs and walk through the markets like a Nigerian woman or a Chinese rice farmer. I was fascinated by the other, and I wanted an unachievable level of closeness.

Presented with the option to live with a local Guatemalan family for the summer in a *very* local village *very* far from the usual tourism pitstop of Lake Atitlan back in college, I signed up with my heart exploding for that kind of experience, which wound up including a lifelong fluency in Spanish, an intestinal parasite that would take me a decade to recover from, and bed bugs. Still, the experience of playing soccer and being teased by the local boys every evening, waking up in the most brightly colored village I had ever seen, and eating dinner with a family who felt, at their core, exactly like my family in Buffalo was a priceless imprint on my nineteen-year-old heart that loved the world and all its colorful people and cultures and longed to know them all.

Later, my shoestring budget came more out of necessity to stay high on the travel drug and stretch my dollars to the next one-way ticket. I took many twenty-hour train rides in India, sleeping in tiny bunks (me to one bed, five Indians to another) and drinking tea the chai *wallahs* hawked in huge containers of questionable hygiene as I was repeatedly and intensely asked where my husband was by the five people with delightfully decorated eyes across the way, the sound of jingling anklets and Bollywood music blaring from someone's cell phone punctuating the long hours in the background.

I would skip taxis and walk home at night from nightclubs in places like

Cairo and Addis Ababa, not the most sensible choice for a lone woman *anywhere* in the world. So, why did I do it? To save the five dollars on the cab, which in local prices would feed me for another day or two on the road. It seemed like a sensible trade-off to the twenty-three-year-old who would give anything to not go back home to a real job for a while. Who still wanted to hitchhike through Burma (did it, and talked three German guys into coming along with me), sleep a night on the Great Wall of China (did it, and I'm pretty sure it's illegal), take a multiday boat trip through the Brazilian Amazon (did it, and learned how to sleep in a hammock for the first time in my life), and "couch surf" through South America (did that too).

Thus, I learned to expertly stretch a dollar through my habits as a backpacker. To save, pinch pennies, sacrifice, and get by with less. It was a badge of honor on the backpacker circuits of South America and Southeast Asia, and it also had origins in my childhood programming around money as well.

When I was growing up, my dad would leave the house before the sun came up, pulling on a blue or brown uniform and various layers of coats, boots, hoodies, and gloves that had borne the weathering effects of Buffalo winters year after year.

Occasionally, I'd be up for school early enough to see him shoveling in some cold cereal and packing a thermos of coffee into his lunchbox before heading out the door. I'd see him again after school when he'd come home, tired and dirty after a day working on roofs and in basements in all climate conditions. We'd always have family dinner together.

It amazes me how he often still found energy to putter around the house on nights and weekends and take on projects that affectionately drove my mother crazy: replacing the roof, building a porch, expanding a room of the house, upgrading the garden.

My dad worked hard. Coming from a family where an alcoholic single mother struggled to put food on the table for her six children, his goal was to provide the stability for me and our family that he never got as a child.

He did that and so much more. He was a loyal provider with a strong work ethic who valued doing the right thing for his family.

He earned about $47,000 per year (as far as I know) and worked his entire life at one of two construction companies. He worked with his body and eventually was forced to retire in his sixties after an injury due to a fall in his older age.

My dad was the earner of the money, and my mom was the stretcher of the money.

She'd sit and clip coupons on Sunday mornings, sipping her coffee and filing each one into an accordion folder that was legitimately twenty years old.

Mom had a system of envelopes in her desk drawer, each one with something like "dinner fund," "Christmas," "gas money," "emergencies," and "church donations" written on the front. Each week she'd go to the bank, deposit my father's paycheck (back in the day), and pull out anywhere from one dollar to twenty dollars to be carefully tucked into their corresponding envelopes.

It was a balancing act.

If we went out to dinner, we could have a $2.19 soda, and it was a treat. Once a year, right before Christmas, we'd go to a fancy restaurant near our house called Salvatore's and order filet mignon and appetizers. I'd gasp while watching mom tuck a crisp $100 bill into the server book with a cheeky and satisfied smile.

She'd reference the sacrifices she had to make and how much she gave up to be able to create those experiences for us.

I was taken to thrift stores to shop for clothes as a kid, but my parents always found enough for the $1,200/year Catholic school tuition.

We never went on vacation, but they did manage to save up and build a brand-new home in a desirable neighborhood inside the best public school district when I was thirteen.

I'm grateful for the values around money I learned as a kid, *and* I had some serious obstacles to overcome if I was going to someday become an entrepreneur and a self-made millionaire.

There were no millionaires in sight growing up.

People in our blue-collar town worked for their paychecks, and they worked hard.

Sacrifices were made and money didn't grow on trees.

Once I learned about "money mindset work," I had my work cut out for me.

I had it ingrained in me to save, not to trust my ability to earn and generate more.
I had watched my parents make the same amount of money for forty years.
I had watched one parent be the breadwinner, the other be the careful financial custodian.
I had learned to put aside money for emergencies and rainy days.
I had learned that there was never a whole lot left over for fun, play, or—now this is crazy rich people talk—*luxury*.

My mom wouldn't even buy strawberries if they were up 40 cents a pound out of season.

Which is how, when I found myself on a call seriously discussing making a $15,000 investment in myself from a "business coach" to learn how to make money online, it was like sending a nun into a strip club. I was way out in uncharted territory.

I'll never forget the day I sat across from my first coach on the screen in my famous moldy Bali bungalow, feeling this incredible hope and wonder at having found someone who was doing exactly what I wanted to be doing.

The first time I met Cait, just a few days prior, she sashayed into a conference room at a coworking space for digital nomads in Bali in a dress

I knew cost at least $200 based on the brand (*luxury* by Bali standards), with a massive amount of dark hair hanging down her back and bright red lipstick on her lips. She was followed by a professional photographer.

She had my attention.

The whole time she facilitated the session for me and the other aspiring online entrepreneurs in the room, I kept thinking, *This woman has made $100,000 doing what I had been doing for the last five years without making more than a few thousand dollars, tops.* Clearly, I had something to learn.

My eyes popped out in wonder.

My eyes popped out even further when I learned that she charged $15,000 to work with her as a private coach for six months.

The hell?

And people paid it. Lots of people.

I'm so proud of myself that in that moment, I didn't write her off. I didn't judge. I allowed myself to be expanded. I allowed myself to feel the possibility.

I allowed myself to see myself in her.

And I amazed myself even more. By the end of the session, I had scribbled about four pages of notes and found myself strolling up to the tall brown-haired beauty and asking about how I could work with her on my "business."

My spine had been healed, my emotions released, my fear and stagnation pacified. I had tried for long enough on my own, my heartbreaking $194 launch included. I was done, and I could finally acknowledge that I needed help. And something about this felt good, like exactly what I needed that I'd never thought of before then. (Coaches? Mentors? High-ticket sales? Not where I come from.)

I stood up straight, booked a call with the woman who deemed herself worthy of $15,000 clients, and I deemed myself worthy to be one.

Never mind that I didn't have $15,000.

Well, not nearly. I had about $12,000 to my name at the time, the glorious net worth of a twenty-nine-year-old woman who'd spent an entire **decade of her life traveling the world, finding her purpose**, obtaining and quitting jobs she didn't really belong doing, all while ignoring the clawing of her soul's true purpose at the edges of her throat and heart.

The $12,000 was hidden in a credit union in Buffalo that I would need to personally go to if I wanted to extract the money. I had set this up on purpose to keep myself from spending my little nest egg on more one-way plane tickets and hippie wanderings.

I had some common sense indeed. It was my version of one big white envelope with "buying time" scrawled on the front of it.

The way I viewed money at that time was a simple calculation: depending on how cheaply I could live, whatever money I had equaled the number of months of freedom from going back to the work and lifestyle I hated.

I was like a frantic squirrel hoarding her acorns for a never-ending winter.

Spending $1,000 per month in Bali like I was at the time would give me a year of freedom on that $12,000.

A year of freedom . . . or six months with a business coach with no guarantees I'd reap even one dollar of profit from my failing business?

With a money mindset like that, it was a miracle I was even considering another way of doing things.

The river of my free-flowing, carefree twenties had dried up and come to a screeching halt. I had healed my body, opened my mind by living on an island full of entrepreneurs, and slammed the door on my former corporate career after getting tossed out of Uber on my ass.

Something big had to happen to change things up, heal my bloodline of struggling Sicilian Americans, and course-correct my destiny.

On that fateful call, when Cait saw my eyes bugging out at the price tag but my heart calling out so desperately for the support, she shared one little story that changed everything.

She shared that her mom, when Cait was growing up in Maine, wouldn't buy grapes at the grocery store if they were up seven cents a pound. Now she was in a position to buy the proverbial grapes and have everything else she desired, and for her family, too.

I thought of my mom and the strawberries. The white envelopes. The once-a-year steak dinners. Tears welled up in my eyes for all the sacrifices and all the women who had denied themselves and played small, me standing on the shoulders of all of them who brought me to this moment where I had an opportunity and choice to do it differently.

I was done.

"I'm in," I said. And then scrunched up my face and crossed my eyes to try to see who it was that had just said that.

I hung up the phone, signed a contract for the $2,500 monthly payment plan option before I could change my mind (remember, I had made about $194 in my business that year and was surviving on $1,000 per month), and shot off an email to the freelance companies I worked part time for and asked for twice the number of clients.

I'd make it work. A new era where Elaina Giolando would make a living doing what she loved was about to begin.

This would also be a good moment to explain how and when Elaina Giolando became Elaina Ray.

As soon as I knew I was committed to this path, I felt I needed a brand name. Giolando is my family name and is still the name in my passport, but it's clunky and hard to pronounce. I have an international lifestyle, and I knew I'd have the clientele to go with it, so I needed something that would flow off the tongue and be instantly recognizable.

I had also spent enough time living in Bali and India where it was common to change one's name. In India, newly christened yoga teachers begin going by their yogic names. My teacher gave me the name Yog Ganga, but I never felt called to use it outside of the ashram. (Guruji has a mind like a steel trap. When I walked into the ashram after a year and thousands of students since he'd seen me, he smiled and wiggled his head in my direction: "Yog Ganga!") In Bali, we'd laugh about the straight-laced guy who would land here and within six months be wearing all white, walking around with a turban on his head, and calling himself Krishna. The women would arrive as Michelle from Chicago and leave as Kali Aurora from the Pleiades, or something just as ridiculous.

"Ray" came from the first time I went home after moving to Bali and got very excited about one of my many money-making schemes (before dropshipping died and I woke up, as previously discussed).

I decided I'd bring home truckloads of purses and textiles from Ubud and sell them in Buffalo. Surely the exotic goods would be a hit in upstate New York. My best friend from high school was on board with the plan and the brand we came up with was Calluna & Ray. Calluna was the genus name for Heather, my friend's name, and Ray she made up because Elaina means "ray of light" in Greek.

I loved the brand name.

Unfortunately for our friendship, the scheme fizzled out quickly, and I went back to Bali with no further intentions of becoming an export-import mule.

But Ray stuck.

Months later, as I embarked on hiring a new web designer and committed to moving away from my old brand, Life Before 30, I decided it was time to come out as Elaina Ray, coach and entrepreneur.

It wasn't easy for me to invest in myself in the way I describe here, by the way. I had just simply come to the realization that I wasn't going to magically understand overnight how to make money from my online business. I didn't know how, and I knew I needed to do what the most successful people in any industry do: learn from someone who's done it before.

The biggest trap I see newer entrepreneurs fall into when they come into my world is saying something like "I'll just wait until I have a few more clients before I hire you" or "I'll just need to 'manifest' the money for this course first before I invest in it," all of which makes zero sense.

If you don't know how to make money in your business or attract clients, and you haven't done so already, what magic is going to occur to change that overnight? Not even reading this book is going to do that for you. You're going to need to go first. You're going to need to pull resources from other means and funnel them into the business in order to capacitate yourself to run it in a profitable way.

This is what entrepreneurs in any other industry do: They raise money to get their businesses off the ground. They don't expect a new product idea to generate capital, they pull capital from somewhere else and use it to support the product to come to life and get traction in the market. Even as a personal brand, you need to do the same.

When potential clients tell me they are considering getting a second job or taking out a loan to work with me, I say, "Great. Smart move." I did the same here, as you've found out. I worked double time at my matchmaking job and took on extra yoga classes and whatever else I could come up with to be able to pay my business coach. I didn't have $15,000 to pay her when I signed up. I also knew I could not expect my business to produce $15,000 before it was ready in order to pay for the coaching I needed to get me to the point where I could produce that kind of money from my business.

There was a period of transition when my extra jobs financed the business. I didn't expect the business to finance my life before I had invested in its ability to do so. Do not make the mistake of using insubstantial logic that will delay you ever getting your business off the ground in the way you desire. You're going to have to invest in it first before you see the results. That takes guts, faith, and a true entrepreneurial spirit. Which is what is required.

As for how I found and chose my first coach (and how I still choose my mentors today), I go wherever I feel led and guided, and I completely trust that guidance. For nearly every one of my coaches, I have known them personally or been referred to them through my network, and then upon seeing their livestreams and feeling their energy and personality via their social media accounts, I fell in love and knew I needed to develop a relationship with that person and be taught by them. I could see they had things set up in their businesses that I wanted too, and I knew even closing a tiny gap in the way I did sales based on a piece of their strategy or upleveling my marketing even a tiny bit with the help of their expert eyes would produce a wild multiplication of the results in my own business.

Most of all, I saw myself in them. I knew that if they could do it, so could I. I saw them as inspiring and impressive, but not that different from me. That feeling of resonance allowed me to attain my results faster because they didn't seem impossible or out of reach or exclusively for some different breed of human. They seemed achievable for me, exactly as I was.

My coaches have all helped me become a better coach too. I know I can teach, hold space, and serve as a leader because I received world-class coaching from them, and I participated in top-level programs as a client. I learned by osmosis and from following their good example.

This is one of the most important intrinsic benefits I know I'm going to receive whenever I hire a new coach: I will get a very tangible upgrade in how I'm able to show up for *my clients* because I invested in myself. Because I'm constantly choosing to evolve and learn from more experienced mentors, the people learning from me get better results and my whole business goes on an upward spiral. Clients get better results, leave better testimonials, rave about my work even more, and bring in even more and even better high-level clients just like them who I'm even better capacitated to serve, which means I can hire higher-level mentors and the cycle continues. See the endless positive upward momentum that generates?

HOMEWORK FOR THIS CHAPTER

1. List out five names of people who have the results you want in an area of your life you're desiring growth or change in. For each one, describe how you see yourself in them. Where are you a lot alike? If they can do it, so can you.

2. What is one investment you know you need to make now that you've been hesitating on? Imagine the you twelve months from now who is already at the place you want to be. What would that version of you do about this investment decision? How would he or she make it?

3. What are three moves you don't feel ready to make yet in your business? What results do you think you would get if you just decided to do them now before you feel "ready?"

4. Picture the version of you who is living twelve months into the future and has everything you want. Ask: "What did you do to get there? Tell me the story of how it happened looking back from where you are now."

CHAPTER 6

PRESSING PLAY

UBUD, BALI, INDONESIA
MARCH 21, 2019

I paced nervously around my simple room three times clockwise, palms sweating, chanting my go-to mantra for strength under my breath. I looked a *little* neurotic you might say.

Peering over my upstairs terrace with a simple wooden table and chair with a tripod, I could see a colorful jungle garden below with a small fishpond. The moldy bungalow was cheap, but also charming.

I sat on the chair, sighed loudly enough for my neighbors to hear, and hovered my finger over the "Go Live" button.

And stopped.

Then went back to pacing.

Correction. *Totally* neurotic.

This was a big moment, though. My coach and I had established that I'd need to produce more social media content, not just the blogs I had been doing up until that point on Life Before 30, and I knew that video was going to be the way I'd reach my first big clients.

In reality, anybody paying over $500 would be a "big" client at that point.

I had seen other people who did their own thing online doing livestreams on Facebook, and I often sat transfixed by their confidence and ability to speak without a script. What I loved most was the casual, low-key celebrity vibe where I got to see them on location in incredible places around the world, cracking jokes, and talking to the camera like I was right there with them.

Growing up, I often imagined that I was being followed around by a camera crew for my own TV show. I quite literally grew up dancing on stage. I became a competitive cheerleader in my teens, and I even did theater in high school. I couldn't hit a ball to save my life, but I was made for the spotlight.

Becoming a coach seemed like the perfect way to get paid to take up space, talk about whatever I wanted, and help people along the way. My dream career path was crystal clear, but I was still nervous about stepping into that role.

How would my old community from IBM and New York City react to Elaina in Bali becoming a life coach? Didn't she used to wear suits and meet presidents for a living? Now she's a barefoot corporate dropout trying to give other people advice on Facebook?

What would my high school guidance counselor think?

Would anyone take me seriously? Did I even take myself seriously?

And more important than my fragile ego and the anticipated judgments from probably all of five random people from my past was a deeper fear: *Would anyone out there actually listen to me? Could it work?*

Ultimately, I believed so. I already saw it working for so many other people like me, and I was essentially no different than they were. The thrill of performance, the desire to share the wisdom I knew I had in me, and the longing to be seen and heard by more people than the few hundred readers of my blog brought me to my senses.

I sat down, fixed my hair one last time, and pressed play before I could think twice.

I don't remember what I said in that first livestream, but I know it was like going on an incredible first date and coming home feeling like I had met "the one." Like no one else would ever matter again.

I pressed play and never stopped.

In the first weeks, I shared almost every day. I set myself up with various backdrops, leveraging my Bali location to drum up the audience's interest with palm trees, rice terraces, and temples in the background.

I'd dress up and try to look my best with the basic hippie clothes I had at the time, adding in a flourish of bright red lipstick to stand out on the newsfeed.

Whatever I felt passionate about, I shared. I taught meditation techniques, talked about emotional intelligence, spoke about overcoming fear, told my story about why I moved to Bali, and at the end of almost every video, I shared about my 1:1 coaching program.

Most of all, I enjoyed the process.

At first, no one tuned in to my livestreams. Or one random classmate from literally sixth grade would come on for two minutes and awkwardly hop off, leaving me with crickets.

I just kept talking like there were people watching.

Slowly, the numbers started to tick up to a dozen people watching live, probably curious what I was up to after so long living in Bali with my LinkedIn profile gathering dust. They'd ask me things, so I started to step more into my expert role, answering their questions, sharing my perspective more and more confidently, and owning my opinions.

And slowly but surely, I started to get inquiries about my coaching.

My first offers were very simple on the outside, but there was a tornado of overcomplication that loved to wreak havoc inside the four walls of my head.

I knew I essentially felt called to serve people who were going through a spiritual awakening, mostly corporate ladder climbers who felt a pang of dissatisfaction and wanted to put a finger on their purpose and create a different life with it.

I spent a lot of hours asking myself questions like: *Should I be a life coach or a spiritual life coach? Should I be a purpose coach? A lifestyle coach?* (Seriously, it's okay if you've done this too. It's a total rite of passage for every online entrepreneur.)

I changed my Instagram headline weekly.

I obsessed over the "About Me" page of my website.

I fiddled with my web copy for more than two of the precious six months I had invested in with my coach.

She would try to drag me away and show me the light, emphatically telling me that my website absolutely did not matter in terms of getting sales (fun fact: some present-day clients of mine have made upward of $200,000 of revenue before ever launching their website), but I am a stubborn Sicilian-blooded woman, and if I want to fiddle with the buttons and colors on my website, fiddle I will.

I remember the rush of adrenaline I felt as I drove my scooter through the pouring rain to a party at a villa in the jungle where I burst through the doors with excitement, thinking I had come up with three main pillars of my work. A moment of EUREKA! where everything finally made sense to me.

Drum roll, please.

Courage.
Confidence.
And connection to self.

Oh, dear. I had learned nothing (yet) about standout marketing and good branding.

There were countless stories like this.

I'd bring all these ideas to my incredibly patient coach, but as soon as the words came out of my mouth, it all sounded like the utter nonsense you might scribble half-blind onto a napkin mid-mushroom journey and then earnestly try to explain to your friend soberly the next morning as if the next Gene Keys had been revealed to you and only you.

This is all perfectly normal at this stage of the game, by the way. I had made less than $10,000 with my largely unproven business idea, so we were in the full trial-and-error zone.

I finally came up with the title "self-mastery coach," and that felt big. It felt like an identity that represented the combination of inner work, personal growth, emotional intelligence, and general motivation and life coaching work I was passionate about.

What I love about being an entrepreneur is that everything is self-proclaimed at the beginning stages. You just make shit up as you go, donning yourself with titles and expertise that only you are aware of at first. It takes a lot of balls to declare "I'm an expert at self-mastery" to the world.

And that's precisely what I did.

My first proper package was three months for $1,500. I worked on it with my coach, but I still felt blocked asking for that much money for just four sessions per month. Even though I was paying nearly double that myself for coaching, I didn't believe I had enough value to offer for that price. Having only ever sold one-off, sixty-minute sessions up until that point, I struggled to think about what we'd even talk about for so long.

I'll never forget the response I got from one man in Kentucky who reached out to me about coaching. When I shared my rates (and I think I even lowballed it and said it was $600 for a month), he responded back completely livid.

"$600?! Who do you think you are? Lawyers don't even charge that much. And you're living in Indonesia, I see. This all seems very fishy, like you have some criminal background and had to run away. I've got connections at the FBI. You better believe I'm going to call them up and have them look into you. You better be careful charging like that."

I felt a knife reach through the screen and stab me in the stomach. My heart pounded. I felt so invaded and genuinely terrified.

Had I done something wrong?

I didn't have my business registered yet as an LLC. *Could I get in trouble for soliciting sales online without that?*

My head spun.

I officially had my first hater and borderline threat on my life, and I was only weeks into my formal coaching career. This was my worst nightmare.

Thankfully, I had a mentor and a support system of fellow entrepreneurs in Bali to share this story with, and my sharing it out loud with them took the charge out of it. I could even laugh about it.

I wound up blocking the guy and getting the inspiration to turn it into a post. "Someone threatened to call the FBI on me because my life seems so impossibly good" became one of my most popular posts back then. My fans rallied behind me, thinking it was hilarious that the guy was so off base that he couldn't even imagine a woman like me having a life where I could legitimately charge whatever I wanted in my own business, live in paradise, and have a potent voice online simply because I decided to show up.

The clients came, one by one.

First, a package for $600 for four sessions. Then, an $800 client for two months (paid my rent!), and, as my confidence grew, I worked myself up to selling the $1,500 package.

I realized fairly quickly how good I was, how fast my clients were getting results, and that I was horrendously undercharging. Then I sold several $2,500 offers as well.

Ironically, the clients who paid more got better results. They were easier to work with and more committed, and I discovered that I even coached better in those sessions (and my rates these days range from ten to a hundred times those original baby coach prices with seas of satisfied clients).

> I CREATED EVERYTHING I HAVE TODAY SIMPLY BY BEING WILLING TO GET ON THE INTERNET, START A LIVESTREAM, TEACH THE PEOPLE WHAT I KNOW, TELL THE PEOPLE ABOUT HOW I COULD HELP, AND GIVE THE PEOPLE A WAY TO PAY ME FOR IT. OVER AND OVER AGAIN.

With testimonials from happy customers coming in and the ability to land clients that paid five months of rent in a single go, I was officially free. I'd never have to go back to a corporate paycheck again. I'd never have to answer to anyone else and settle for writing inspiring things that made my heart sing on nights and weekends while pimping out my limited time and energy to busy work that made someone else rich and felt pointless and soul crushing.

My worst fear was over.

In a nutshell, I created everything I have today simply by being willing to get on the internet, start a livestream, teach the people what I know, tell the people about how I could help, and give the people a way to pay me for it. Over and over again. Today, that is still how I make my money and run my business. I prioritize teaching, doing live video, and revealing what's inspiring for me on a daily basis to my audience.

The hardest part was getting out of my own way to do that by deciding I did have something to say and valuing what I had to say first. Of course no one was interested in what I had to say when I first started. Of course I had to try really hard to get even ten people to sign up for a free workshop I hosted. Of course people ignored my posts and emails at the beginning. But I chose to keep going. I kept sharing, posting, teaching, and emailing, and over time, little by little, more people noticed. More people found value in what I was sharing as I grew to share it more and more confidently. Your people will do the same. We all start at zero. We all start with no followers, no loyal fans except our mom and perhaps, our partner. You generate your momentum by believing in yourself first and relentlessly putting your gifts out there.

I recently launched a free training and 400 people signed up practically overnight, a new record for me. My Facebook group now has 2,000 people in it. When I started, no one signed up for even my free masterclasses. There were fifteen people in my Facebook group. I was a nobody. I grew it one person at a time, one training at a time, one course at a time, one video at a time, one chance taken on myself at a time. I showed up. Consistently. Every single day. Even when nobody was watching or clapping or cheering me on. I showed up for me. For my vision. And I hope you do the same.

If you're feeling some nervousness around putting yourself out there and joining this industry of self-appointed authorities, you're in perfect company. I've never worked with anyone out of the thousands of clients and course students I've served who was super comfortable from the get-go with pressing play and preaching their wisdom to the random people of the internet. They had me to support them for a reason.

Here's one of my favorite activities to get unblocked around visibility in your brand. Take out a piece of paper and draw a line down the middle.

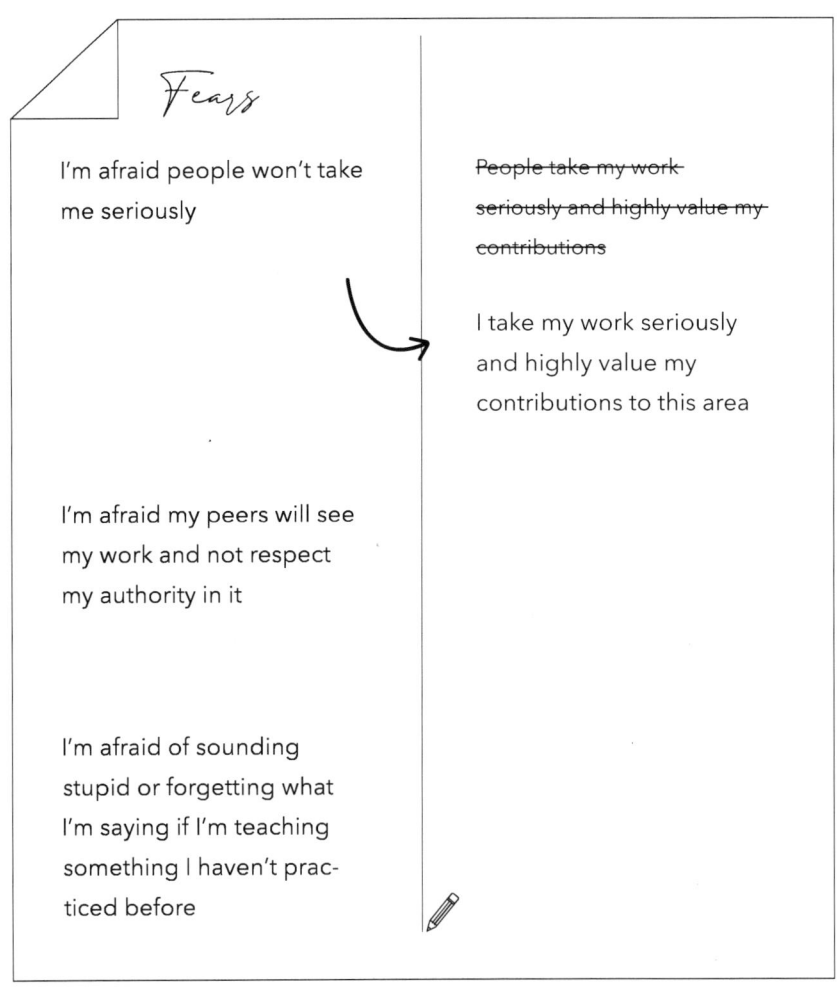

- On the left side, write out all the fears you have around being seen. Things like "I'm afraid people won't take me seriously," "I'm afraid my peers will see my work and not respect my authority in it," "I'm afraid of sounding stupid or forgetting what I'm saying if I'm teaching something I haven't practiced before," etc.

- On the right side, write a statement that disproves every fear and doubt you just listed. Continue until you have rewritten each of your statements and corrected these fears to something you want to believe instead and that feels better in your body.

- But here's the key. Notice on the left side how many statements contain things about other people or used the pronouns "he, she, they, people."

- When you consider that opposite way of looking at it and write your corrected statement on the right, you want to use exclusively the "I" pronoun. For example, you might be tempted to correct "I'm afraid people won't take me seriously" to "People take my work seriously and highly value my contributions." *That is not what you want to do.* The better option is to center the new belief and story on yourself, which sounds like "I take my work seriously and highly value my contributions to this area."

- Do that for every single item on the list, then rip the paper in half, burn the left side, and hang the right side up in your office.

- Each day, read it over for a few minutes of daily mindset work that will get you grounded in what is within *your* control to choose to believe and how you can show up for yourself, which is what becoming self-made is built on. You show up for you. Every day.

Here's a secret about how I do livestreams, even today: I tend to do them right after client calls when I'm feeling inspired about a topic my clients and I were jamming on that I think is relevant to a wider audience. If I do any preparation at all, I'll take out a sticky note, jot down a few talking points, and keep the note on my desk. Then I just get out the camera and riff. I pretend like I'm catching up with a friend on the amazing thing I just discovered relevant to the work I do, or I'll summarize an answer to a great question someone asked on a mastermind call. At the end of the riff, I let people know what programs I have open and how they can work with me. I always warmly invite them to reach out and DM me if they have any questions about which offer might be the right level of support for them. Yes, I sell on every single video I ever do. It would be rude not to offer people the opportunity to get the transformation in this area the way my clients are.

Here's why this works. First, if the content idea came from a current ideal client, it is likely to be relevant to hundreds if not thousands of other people just like that person who already found me, paid me, and is getting value from our work together. Second, the more natural, the less rehearsed, the less premeditated video content looks and is, the more **magnetic it is to your audience.** They feel like they get to know you at a personal level this way, which builds the know, like, and trust factor.

Sometimes I'll even do live videos walking through Bali, sitting next to or in my pool, or being on the go in some way to give people a sense of my organic lifestyle that the transformational journey I've been on has provided me.

Pricing your offers. As far as pricing, my go-to recommendation is to price based on the lifetime value of your offers, not an hourly rate. For example, my mastermind and private coaching offers are five- and multiple-five-figure investments. I don't price based on the number of sessions or even the number of months of the program's mentorship. I price based on the skills I teach capacitating my clients to be able to earn five and even six figures per month for the rest of their lives when they learn and implement what I teach them. Their lifetime earning potential exponentially increases from working with me, and my fee is simply a very small part of that investment up front.

This advice is valid for any niche, even if you do nothing when it comes to business or money-making activities. If you're a relationship coach, the work you do to reprogram how someone relates to men or women will shape every interaction they have relationally for the rest of their life. If you're a healer, unblocking someone's core wounds or self-sabotage will increase the success they have in every aspect of their life, including their career and earning potential, for the rest of their life. If you're a personal trainer, teaching someone how to work with their body will change how they look and feel for the rest of their life. If you're a health coach, the way someone shifts their thoughts around food will change how they experience every meal for the rest of their life, not to mention help them avoid costly health issues in the future. The tools you teach, no matter what niche you're in, stay with a client far beyond the duration of the container you support them in, and the lifetime value of those upgrades in how someone experiences things like sex, relationships, their health, food, friendship, parenthood, money, and their purpose for decades to come is extremely high.

I also know that price is a filter for money mindset, self-worth, self-belief, and general life experience that I need the client to come in with before we start working together if they are going to be ready to implement and take action at the level I require them to in order to be successful. If someone is scared to invest in themselves because they are worried they'll never make back the money or they don't trust their ability to make money period, those are introductory concepts and foundational work I don't personally teach or desire to support someone with but are essential for success in the business world. I teach some of those principles in a few self-study courses or low-ticket products and then only take clients at my higher levels of coaching who understand how investments work, who know and believe that every dollar they spend on themselves comes back tenfold, and trust themselves enough to do the work, take messy action, and see results over time.

Self-trust and trust in life itself working out are important things to learn, and some coaches will absolutely be very successful teaching on those topics, but they simply lie outside *my* primary zone of genius, which is taking someone who has full faith in the possibility for huge business success being imminently available to them and teaching them the skills around management, marketing, and sales that will get them there swiftly. For you, too, there are foundational concepts that lie outside your immediate zone of genius, and you'd be better off letting someone work with a different coach or take introductory courses on personal development before working with you so you save space in your practice for the individuals who are already ready to move and get results. *Plus*, you get to stay in your absolute zone of genius when it comes to your work. For more information on pricing, please see the Resources.

To niche or not to niche? The last piece here is around niching. As a new entrepreneur, this was one area I got lost in overanalyzing and looping around. I made it way more complicated than it needed to be. Essentially, you're not going to get it right from the beginning, so don't even worry about trying. Instead, literally take the best guess you have at a niche and go full out and full blast: launch offers, write lots of content, and film videos, and based on who shows up on your sales calls and how much you like the work you get from that niche attempt, you'll pivot accordingly. The biggest reason you'll fail is not because your niche isn't "correct" or good enough but because you'll never start, be as loud and proud as you need to be, or sell boldly enough.

I tell my clients to think of niche as a *conversation you'll be having on the internet* instead of a specific type of person you're serving. Contrary to what most marketing experts say, your niche according to me is not a person, but a clear outcome and transformation you provide. In my case, I don't work with a specific type of entrepreneur and keep myself boxed in. I am highly skilled at helping people grow million-dollar online businesses, so if that outcome resonates with them, they can seek me out.

Everyone from coaches to healers and therapists to architects, artists, and other service providers (even brick-and-mortar owners) come knocking on my door. Why? Because my content and social media presence establishes my clear expertise on messaging, brand positioning, premium sales, team management, and success mindset, and my ideal clients readily see how they could use those skills in their own lives.

> FOR NOW, ASK YOURSELF THIS: IF I KNEW I WAS GOING TO BE SUCCESSFUL NO MATTER WHAT I CHOSE TO FOCUS ON, WHO I SERVED, OR WHAT MY NICHE WAS, WHAT WOULD I CHOOSE? THEN GO WITH THAT.

Think about it in those terms and then be perfectly selfish about it. Pick something *you* love to talk about. Pick a transformation you love to provide and witness people go through. Pick something that feels inspiring and exciting to you now and know that without exception it will change six to twelve months from now. I started out as a career coach, then became a self-mastery and life coach, then a business coach for new coaches, then a business coach for successful coaches ready to scale. Now I work as a high-level business consultant and success mentor for entrepreneurs of all levels and industries ready to go big. Heck, I'm *still* changing and pivoting and tweaking my messaging and positioning because I'm always evolving.

It's a process that never stops because you're in an organic business that's more like an art than a science. You're an artist and a shape-shifter, and your business will need to evolve to keep up with you. That, in fact, is the recipe for success that we'll talk about later in the book. Let the business evolve along with you. It's not meant to be static because you'll outgrow it and it'll flop, and not because the niche isn't perfect but because you stopped loving what you're doing and talking about and creating.

For now, ask yourself this: If I knew I was going to be successful no matter what I chose to focus on, who I served, or what my niche was, what would I choose? Then go with that.

Literally, go with the first thing that comes to mind. Do not overthink it. Niching usually isn't a strategy issue, it's a mindset issue, and you've got to get out of the habit of thinking that one choice will lead to you being successful and another will lead to imminent failure. Whatever you choose to sell and whoever you choose to serve, people are buying *you*, so keep the focus on showing up and revealing who you are and the wisdom you contain. Please visit the Resources for more information on niching and creating your first offer.

HOMEWORK FOR THIS CHAPTER

1. If you couldn't get it wrong, mess it up, or derail the success you know you're meant to have in any way, what would you be doing right now in your business?

2. What would you charge for your services if you couldn't get it wrong, piss anyone off, lose clients, or otherwise steer yourself off the course of your rightful success? What do you need to do to get behind it and back yourself to sell at that number?

3. What is the conversation you really want to be having on the internet with your audience and your clients?

4. Go do a livestream today. Don't prepare any more than three bullet points on a sticky note. Make connecting with your audience and revealing yourself and your wisdom the priority. Be natural and uncensored. How can ideal, soul-mate clients show up if you don't show your quirks and beam your true essence out into the world for them to be attracted to you and find your work, which is the exact thing they've been praying for as a solution to a problem or unmet desire in their own lives?

5. Do your visibility unblocking homework. List out all the stories you're telling yourself about what you're scared about happening if you become more visible and anchor back into what you're choosing to be true for you. Stay in your own lane, which means not trying to control how anyone else responds to what needs to come out of you for your own sake.

CHAPTER 7

FALLING IN LOVE

MOLKOM, SWEDEN
JULY 29, 2019

I felt horribly unprepared.

It was freezing cold, and I had on a thin T-shirt and flip-flops. The tent I'd rented had partially collapsed on me, and I was hauling a heavy blow-up mattress through the forest, trying to make my home for the next week.

I'd felt a distinct soul-calling to Europe that summer. Boarding the plane to Germany from Bali, I had a hunch that it might have something to do with my business starting to get traction. Perhaps I'd discover clients or go on a speaking tour or network with someone important in Berlin, one of my many second homes around the world.

Little did I know that I'd spontaneously book myself a ticket to a "tantra festival" in Sweden and need last-minute bloody camping gear. I was making what I felt to be real money by this point, and roughing it like I did in my backpacker years was becoming less and less appealing.

Shivering, I dropped the mattress in frustration, a tiny bit in diva mode, and trekked to the café where 1,000 young people from all over the world mingled. I didn't know anyone, but I felt excited about participating in a week-long residential festival that was drug free, alcohol free, and centered on both spirituality and sensuality.

I also secretly hoped to meet a guy. (Truth be told, I posted a Facebook status on my flight from Berlin to Stockholm that said cheekily, "Off to meet my future husband!" Totally kidding of course.)

Truthfully, I wanted to meet a really nice, spiritual man who practiced the same kind of yoga and tantra I had learned in India years ago that transformed my life.

I had been single for *nine years*, and besides being broke and clueless about business, which I'd finally rectified, I was utterly hopeless and heartbroken over my perpetual, never-ending state of singlehood.

Back in Bali, I did a morning practice almost every single day where I chanted mantras, meditated, and did every form of healing and energy work to try to call in a man. *I'm ready for him, I swear! Tell me what I need to do,* I'd pray earnestly to an eclectic variety of Christian and Hindu gods . . . and hear nothing. I even regularly prayed to my future husband's guides, introducing myself like an awkward diplomatic envoy to far-reaching parts of the Congo.

Hi, guides of my future beloved. My name is Elaina. I'd like you to know that I already love this person who you also love very much. I understand you have plans for him. He must be in another relationship or learning important lessons right now before he becomes my husband, and I totally respect that. Everything in your timing. Andddd anytime you want to hurry up and steer him in my direction, I'd be very glad. Thank you. Bye for now.

Then I'd go to events and look around the room, checking out every man there and wondering which one was available for me to potentially connect with.

I reeked of desperate energy. Naturally, nothing worked.

Now, scanning through the crowd at Ängsbacka, I suddenly felt incredibly alone and shy. There seemed to be a buzz between people who already knew each other, many couples even, and I wondered if this would be one long, torturous week for single ol' me.

Standing among the chaos, I locked my panicked eyes with a curly haired, warm bubble of energy with big brown eyes. Somehow, my feet carried me until I was standing in front of him, smiling and instantly babbling.

I sheepishly shared about how badly my tent situation was going. I explained that I had just flown in from Bali and didn't realize what a Swedish summer climate would be like. Finally, I blurted out, "What's your name?"

He smiled a huge smile and sparks were most certainly flying.

"You don't remember me?" he teased. "I was in Bali earlier this year. I said hi to you at a few parties and even messaged you on Facebook to ask you out on a date. You turned me down. I'm René."

I vaguely remembered . . . but this couldn't be the same guy?

This man in front of me felt so kind, sweet, and open. The man who asked me out in Bali seemed like a tourist playboy on the prowl. Even as I was chanting my mantras and praying for a man, I turned him down because I was looking for something serious, not another three-week fling with a guy who didn't know what country he was headed to next (I'd had my fill of those types of encounters, especially given my nomadic history).

Just as my mind was racing to put the pieces together, a tall blonde woman appeared at his side. Our smiles faded, and he shifted awkwardly.

"This is my girlfriend," he said as he put his arm around her waist.

Well, this wouldn't be going anywhere now either. *All the good ones are taken*, I confirmed, disappointed, then excused myself to get a chai.

Later that night, I settled into my tent alone, exhausted from the flight from Germany plus a four-hour bus ride through rural Sweden. I threw on socks with my flip-flops and every possible layer of clothing I could find.

Peeking out of my tent, I saw a curly haired figure wandering down the forest path, a cozy Moroccan-style sweatshirt pulled adorably over his head. He was holding a big gray hoodie in his hands.

Looking for someone, it appeared.

As he approached, he smiled again. "I brought this for you. You mentioned you were cold, and I thought you could use this tonight."

The short version of a long story is that René and I fell in love over the course of those four days in Ängsbacka. He broke up with the girlfriend, asked me to be with him, and I blurted out yes, unthinking, yet deliriously happy.

Coincidentally and conveniently, he was already planning to move to Bali from his home in the Netherlands. The stars had aligned. My guides and his had apparently made a peace treaty and decided to move along the inevitable declaration of sacred interdependence.

I still had almost no memory of meeting him back in Bali the previous January, but he swore that the world stood still the first time he saw me, all dressed in white, at a sober full-moon party. I was apparently standing alone in the middle of the dance floor, swiveling my head around like an owl, undoubtedly checking out every man in the room for potential relationship material.

Blind. Deaf. Missing the point.

Missing the only man who would matter.

Having René as my partner has influenced and improved every part of my life since we met. Feeling loved and accepted by someone so deeply has provided a safe base to continue to put myself out there and grow my business, so it's no coincidence that from this moment in my story, my results absolutely skyrocketed. Some psychologists refer to healthy long-term relationships as "background objects"—a term usually used to refer to how a very young child in their first two years of life views the mother as a background object. Just by knowing she's there, the child has

> THE WANTING I FELT FOR SOMETHING WAS DIRECTLY CONNECTED TO THAT SOMETHING WANTING ME ON THE OTHER END OF THAT ENERGETIC THREAD OF THE UNIVERSE.

the confidence to take her first steps out into the world. Healthy romantic partnership provides this same kind of safety for adults, knowing that we have a base of unconditional love and support from which to explore ourselves, our purpose, and the world around us. When we have healthy romantic relationships that foster a sense of support, safety, and love, we feel as though we can conquer anything.

But let me not give my power over to the relationship, as it fundamentally isn't about that. It's about the huge boost of personal power I experienced from finally being able to obtain something I truly desired and healing one of my core wounds that told me the lie that I couldn't have it. I healed the scarcity story around love and men, and I used my own rituals, prayer, and a hell of a lot of inner work and personal development to call it in. I decided. I decided that if it was available to other women, then there was no reason that big, epic love and a committed, emotionally available man should not be available for me as well. I decided that if I desired this kind of relationship that it meant it was destined for me and it was in my highest good. I stopped doubting that I would get what I wanted and gave into the knowing that the wanting I felt for something was directly connected to that something wanting me on the other end of that energetic thread of the universe.

I believe there is a strong and direct connection between love, money, and purpose. Often, clients who move through my masterminds and private coaching will begin single, with their business underperforming and then leave with a partner and having multiplied their bottom lines. The sense of self-worth, deservingness, and letting it be good and letting it be easy and letting yourself have it because it's available are all core concepts that we work on. The energetic shift is so profound and so essential to the way this person moves in the world that men, money, and other opportunities can't help but take note and simply fall into place. (Visit the Resources for a link to see me teach live about my manifestation of partnership and how love, money, and business are all interconnected.)

Here are the essential concepts I teach women who come to me interested in knowing exactly how I manifested my partner after nine years of being single and having a lot of wounding around whether love would be available or possible for me.

1. **Separateness and specialness.** I challenged every part of myself that bought into the idea of separateness on some level, which looked like seeing women who had a committed partner and thinking of all the ways she was different from me, better than me, or had it easier than me. The truth is, if I thought I was so special that love couldn't find me in the way I desired it, I would find every way to be right about that, consciously or unconsciously. If I chose to see myself in every happily married woman and see her as no different from me, having had her trials and tribulations and doubts about whether she could have it too and then getting it, I could celebrate her love as my own and trust that if I was not separate or special, I would have it as well.

2. **High standards and clear boundaries.** I practiced celibacy for almost a year before I met René, and it is the number one thing that almost all my close friends who are married or happily partnered say they did to call in their sacred union. They may have dated around, had options, and stayed unattached during the dating process like mainstream relationship coaches will tell you to do, but they did not get into bed until they were in a relationship and had found their man. In the end, René and I didn't sleep together until six weeks into our relationship. Before that, I didn't allow anyone into my space sexually unless we were exploring genuine long-term connection. Sounds old fashioned and maybe harsh or crazy and hard to do, but it worked. It didn't come from the space that traditional dating experts would tell women to do this from, but rather it came from a genuine space of me knowing I could not compromise my energy or drop my standards or make space for anything at that level of intimacy unless it was exactly what I wanted. It was a full-body *yuck* to settle for only the physical intimacy without the safe container I truly desired around it, which I had done plenty of in the past and knew it never gave me what I wanted. We all know the definition of insanity is doing the same thing over and over again and expecting different results.

3. **I changed my relationship to my longing for love.** The feeling of an unmet need or desire can be so irritating, like an empty ache deep in your bones. Instead of rejecting the sensation of that unmet longing itself and trying to look outward for a solution to make it go away (such as getting a partner) like I had for years prior to this revelation, I was guided with the knowing that embracing the

longing itself somehow held the key to discovering what could manifest on the other side of that energetic thread of desire in the universe. I did a lot of somatic and spiritual work around allowing the desire and longing and ache I felt in my body to bubble up and overwhelm me, feeling its strength and power and soreness, its fire and prickliness. Soon enough, after enough practice holding the feeling, I discovered what it felt like deep underneath it all: raw power. My desire was powerful. I went from victim who wasn't getting a man and asking the universe to show me what I had to do to "fix myself" to get one and pouting and stomping my proverbial spiritual feet like a little brat to an empowered woman in touch with her body and desire, who could roar into the flames of the unmet desire and simply melt with how much she already loved the man she was destined to meet and accept the ravishment of the pain of him not being here yet, with no more doubt or fear or skepticism or pity in the mix whatsoever. Simply a woman who could fully feel what she wanted and how much sensation behind that bigness there was. It wasn't long after some meditations like this that I met my partner.

Not only do these practices work for attracting a partner, but can you see how deciding not to view yourself as separate from the people creating the business results you also want to create, setting clear boundaries and standards and making sure your offers, prices, and clients all match what you truly want (and holding out for it), and then changing your relationship to the longing itself that you feel for results you desire but aren't here yet would catapult you into a completely different level of long-term success?

HOMEWORK FOR THIS CHAPTER

1. What are the clear standards in your business and love life that you are establishing and upholding from now on?

2. Where are you feeling irritated by your desire for a next level that simply isn't here yet? How can you shift the feeling to your desire to something more empowering?

3. Where are you seeing yourself as separate or special and different from the people who have the things you want? Choose one person who has something in business or love that you want for yourself and list all the reasons they are just like you. How can you get into a "if he or she can have it, so can I" attitude about anything you desire?

4. Where are you so blinded by the vision of the future or the thing you want that you're missing the here and now, taking something or someone for granted, or otherwise potentially overlooking exactly the thing you're so desperately searching for "out there?" Is it possible that it's right under your nose after all?

CHAPTER 8

CASTING OFF FROM MY VERY LAST JOB (AND FINDING SAFETY WITHIN)

UBUD, BALI, INDONESIA
NOVEMBER 5, 2019

If I had to talk to one more stubborn, picky, neurotic forty-year-old Manhattan lawyer about how her clock was ticking to meet a good Jewish guy *while* she turned down every suggested date I presented her with, I was going to become the local village nut, wandering around naked in the Balinese jungle, completely unhinged for good.

The contrast between my coaching calls where I was the boss and my work as a part-time matchmaker, which I clung to like a toddler hanging fitfully around her mom's knees on the first day of preschool, was brutal.

By this point, my coaching clients were becoming so self-mastered that they were all quitting their jobs and turning into entrepreneurs and wanting my help with that. Who would have thought I could be a business coach? But that's where the ship was naturally steering me.

The irony was, I just couldn't rip the bandage off the steady part-time work that was bringing me in about $2,500 to $3,000 per month, which was roughly the same as my coaching income back then.

I loved my new career path. I loved how the space I had learned to hold invited the client to roam from revelations about their purpose and relationships to bursts of creative idea generation for the next chapter of their life. I loved their tearful breakthroughs and the feeling of gratitude they had for our work. I felt grateful they trusted me with their time, money, and innermost secrets. We had a blast.

Slowly but surely, however, it was the contrast of being in a so-far-so-steady relationship with a loyal man I already loved and the grating vibration of hearing the doomsday mindset of women desperately hiring an online matchmaking company and yakking my ear off on the other side of the world that became the straw that broke the camel's back.

I could no longer juggle my energy and be divided in two drastically different directions. I could no longer compromise on the hours I had to spend to make a few hundred dollars by setting up dates for people I couldn't relate to anymore. My empathy had reached a breaking point. And I had a hunch that if I freed up the hours I spent matchmaking every week that the extra time devoted to my coaching would bring me more clients.

It was still excruciatingly hard to pull the plug.

I had never actually worked 100 percent for myself in my entire life. I was also thirty years old, and I had made a commitment to myself that I wanted to be my own boss by the time I was thirty. Now was as good of a time as any to claim being a full-time entrepreneur. Even if my monthly income was still sparse, I didn't need a lot to live on. At the end of the day, I was free with what I had already created.

Or I could be free.

In my younger years, I got a job as soon as it was legal for me to start working and found my first gig at the local ice cream shop called Anderson's. The other kids from my class would come in after school and order sandwiches, fries, and soft serve and hang out until soccer practice, while I was the bus girl who wiped down the tables, refilled the ketchup, and hauled the garbage out for $8/hour so I could save up for college.

I wasn't a loser, though. In high school, I was freshman class president, a varsity cheerleader, the president of multiple clubs and organizations, and a top student. Your classic overachiever. After a decade of being an outsider and being bullied by kids since kindergarten, I finally got along with almost everyone, and everyone (I think) liked me for the most part.

And I worked hard.

Every time I worked an Anderson's shift, about three times per week for a few hours, I counted down the hours and stacked my dollars, literally cashing my paychecks and putting the bills in a white envelope underneath my underwear drawer. Every week I scribbled down the number of how much money was inside. Sound familiar?

I saved everything.

Later, I upgraded to working at the popular neighborhood greasy pizza joint as a bus girl, but someone else took out the garbage. All I had to do was pour water, clear tables, and make sure customers had all the condiments their hearts desired. Plus, I got tips if I was nice to the waitresses.

Shifts at Sorrentino's were exhausting, and I always came home reeking of fried oils and pepperoni. I worked there for over two years, doing extra shifts over the summer months to save up more money. The notations on my envelopes grew.

By my senior year of high school, I had saved close to $1,800 cash. My parents didn't have the money to send me to college, something they had informed me of a long time prior, hence the bus-girl hustle. Fortunately, I also got ridiculously good grades and was a strong writer, so my college admissions essays were masterpieces.

So much so that I'll never forget the quiet snowy evening when I got a very strange phone call from a school I had applied to early on a whim, a notoriously difficult school to get into as an out-of-state student: the prestigious University of North Carolina at Chapel Hill. It was the Dean of Admissions. My essay had touched the admissions board so much that they had to ring me up and tell me so, and tell me that I got in, *and* tell me that I was invited to interview as a finalist for a full scholarship.

I wound up flying down to Chapel Hill for the interview, and a few weeks later received the letter that informed me I was the recipient of the Pogue Scholarship, a full-ride, top-tier college education with the value of *$150,000* for four years.

To this day, I bawl my eyes out even thinking about that moment, holding the letter in my shaking hands. As a tender seventeen-year-old with big dreams to study at a top university far away from boring Buffalo, New

York, and smelly restaurant shifts, I was completely in shock and full of gratitude.

That letter was the first big thing in my life that really set me free. Its positive ripple effects changed the entire course of my adult life and certainly supported me to be an entrepreneur sooner because I didn't have the crippling student loan debt I otherwise would have had.

(I used the $1,800 to buy textbooks for a few years, the only things that weren't included in the scholarship. Thank goodness I wasn't determined to save up $150,000 clearing pizza trays before I got my education.)

Why am I sharing this story? Because even after I got a full-ride scholarship to college, I worked all four years.

I saved up a few thousand dollars while in university so that the day I graduated I could fly myself to Buenos Aires on a one-way ticket and backpack solo around South America for three months before starting my first big adult job at IBM Consulting in New York.

I was addicted to working and saving money, just like my parents had done their whole lives. It provided me with a feeling of comfort and control. To me, earning money made me feel safe.

Work, work, work. My whole life had been work.

So, of course, when it came to the moment in Bali when my finger hovered over the send button to quit my last, truly last job ever, after another several years of freelancing and hobbling together dollars from various online gigs, I winced, saved draft, and closed my laptop.

I was still doing the white envelope thing. I had invested $15,000 in myself, made it all back and more, only to realize the nine-to-five, money-makes-me-feel-safe conditioning ran even deeper.

If I was going to really succeed and do this on my own sustainably, I would have to stop relying on money for my feeling of safety. I would have to trust my abilities, my character, my flexibility, and my intuition and feel safe from within, knowing that entrepreneurship offered no guarantees and there might very well be income roller coasters ahead of me.

Finally, one fateful day, I clicked send on the email to the matchmaking company with a prayer and a deep exhale. That was it.

The last cord to my way of being with money since I was fifteen was severed.

Little did I know that severing that cord would skyrocket my business to over $10,000/month right afterward, and just six months later I would have my first $100,000 *month*.

So, this is where I give some input that's a little taboo for typical business coaches to give: There's nothing wrong with having a job to help support you as an entrepreneur. While I was growing my business during the first year, I liked having my part-time jobs because I knew that my needs would be met financially, and I'd never have to take on an unaligned client just to pay the bills or compromise on my prices or offer something I wasn't truly excited about because it seemed like it would "do well" in a launch. The jobs gave space to my business and allowed it to grow organically and in alignment from the beginning without murky "I need money" energy behind any sale or business decision.

SOMETIMES YOUR BUSINESS SIMPLY CAN'T SUPPORT YOU UNTIL YOU'VE INVESTED ENOUGH IN IT AND IN YOURSELF TO LEARN HOW TO MAKE IT GENERATE MONEY FOR YOU.

Here's the thing: Sometimes your business simply can't support you until you've invested enough in it and in yourself to learn how to make it generate money for you. That's one of the biggest things I'll call out in people who approach me wanting to work together but then say something like "Well, I'll just wait to get a few more clients and then I'll hire you." To that I say, "But that's the whole reason you need to hire me first. If you knew how to just magically get more clients, you wouldn't need a business coach. You need to learn the skills it takes to make money on your own from your independent, heart-led business and then you can let it run like a well-oiled machine and provide the same kind of stability (plus much higher numbers) than a job used to provide for you. Until then, don't make the mistake of hoping and wishing for stability from something you haven't set up properly to function at a level that could feasibly bring in consistent money. That's a process and a learned skill."

At the same time, there's something to be said around knowing when to take the risk you know you need to take. Entrepreneurship requires constant risk-taking and cool-headed assessment of risk. The message I want to convey to you here is: **It's safe to trust yourself.** You know. You hear the voice nudging you to let go. You hear the whispers come up that say you've got to step away and cut ties with anything that dilutes your energy and puts your focus on anything other than what you're building for the future. You know you're truly meant to have it all. The bigness, the spotlight, the success, the wealth and power, the soul-fulfilling lifestyle. You'll know when it's a distraction from your purpose and when it's a practical support that's aiding in the ease of establishing what needs to be established.

When the time comes, know that you'll never feel ready, so don't wait for the sensation of readiness in your body. Assess what feels like the right thing to do and trust the intuitive guidance you're receiving. Fear sounds like an alarm blaring or a high-pitched, hyperventilating kind of voice. Intuition is the whisper from your bones, a quieter and more subtler knowing that's simply acknowledging truth. Again, you know when you know and you know what you need to do, so back yourself and do what needs to be done, either in getting a job to support your business or letting go of one to support your fullest expansion.

HOMEWORK FOR THIS CHAPTER

1. Would having another source of income be beneficial for where you are in your journey toward becoming self-made? Is there a way where you may have rejected that option instead of seeing it as valid support to approach the path of entrepreneurship in a sustainable way?

2. If you do currently have a second source of income besides your business, where may there be shame around it that needs to be released and alchemized into full backing and full knowing that it's serving you and supporting you toward your ultimate dreams and desires? (Full disclosure: I have high-performing clients making upward of $50,000/month who also have full-time corporate jobs and choose to do both because they truly enjoy both. There's no one way to be an entrepreneur.)

3. If it's past the point of serving and supporting you and you feel ready to cast off from the safety net of relying on someone else for a paycheck or you're feeling energetically drained by the "means to an end" type of work, set a deadline to get out of that arrangement and step full time into your business. In my case, having a part-time job served me for a long time—until it didn't—and then casting off from that shore of safety was exactly what catapulted me into the next level of big results I knew I was meant for. If you sense this is what might be true for you, trust yourself. You know. It's safe to trust yourself.

CHAPTER 9

LEADING YOURSELF THROUGH THE UNKNOWN: THE YEARS WHERE EVERYTHING SHIFTED

HANOI, VIETNAM
DECEMBER 20, 2019

The first sort-of fight René and I had took place on the side of a Vietnamese highway.

Our motorcycle, which we had just driven nonstop for eight days across northern Vietnam, had run out of fuel five minutes and one wrong turn away from our last hotel before flying back to Bali.

The thing was janky, to say the least. We picked it up in a back alley of Hanoi, passing noisy fish-soup sellers, tea shops with no more than a collection of plastic chairs on the side of the road, and piles of colorful fabrics stacked in tiny storefronts with little stern-looking women sitting in front.

The guys we rented from added a "luggage rack" on the back for us, made of two metal poles held together by rope that fell apart every three days, and I rode sandwiched between René and the poles for a week, up and down unforgiving, unpaved mountain roads.

Don't get me wrong, it was bliss.

I had found a man who loved adventure as much as I did. After we committed to each other, he left Sweden to spend a month driving a motorcycle with a group of men through the Indian Himalayas while I spent two weeks with my best friend in Tuscany, eating cheese and giggling over my newfound love. René finally sold the last of his belongings in the Netherlands and met me in Thailand for a month before moving to Bali.

Vietnam almost broke me, though. The highway was pitch black where our little Honda gurgled to a dead halt and giant eighteen-wheelers screamed past us at 100 mph, terrifyingly close. On the map, it was a thirty-minute mandatory detour to go down the one-way highway to the next ramp to turn around to town and get fuel. We'd have to decide what to do with the bike and who would go get fuel. And let me tell you, Uber does not work in Vietnamese Timbuktu.

All because he missed the godforsaken turn to the hotel.

I was livid. And scared. We wound up deciding to leave the bike—a very risky move, as that part of Vietnam is known for theft—but it was a better alternative than leaving one of us behind to be kidnapped.

After experiencing a week of hillside tribes above the clouds, quaint homestays, and views that stretched over scalloped green landscapes for miles, this was a tough way to end the trip.

Unbeknownst to us, it also ended the world as we knew it.

We made it back to Bali, sure enough, but we had picked up a terrible flu on the connecting flight through Malaysia. It lasted for weeks.

I spent New Year's Eve nursing René and René spent New Year's Day nursing me. Neither of us had ever felt so sick, and neither of us had any idea what we had other than a bug from the airplane.

A few weeks later, I felt a strong knowing exactly like when my soul called me to Sweden. This time it said to go to India, yet another of my "second homes" around the world. I had been every year for three years and just the mention of Rishikesh, my most beloved town on the planet, was enough to make my heart ache for Satsang with my spiritual teachers and dips in the Ganga.

Always up for an adventure, René and I left for India for a month in late January. That was when the news of a strange Chinese virus started to hit the airwaves. I remember going to see Mooji-Baba speak and seeing the Chinese visitors wearing masks there for the first time. There were probably 4,000 people in the hall sitting around, sandwiched like chickens.

Like many people at that time, we dismissed the coronavirus as something far away, an unfortunate problem for an isolated part of China. I was excited for my new beloved to meet Guruji in the ashram where I stayed for four months the previous year and to bathe in the holy Ganges River together.

I was also in the middle of a $60,000 launch, taking sales calls while looking over the iconic red bridges with temples stacked on the riverbanks, the whole town overflowing with devotees from around India and the world. It was an epic way to make money: traveling the world with my love, putting myself through my annual spiritual washing machine, and selling out my first business mastermind.

Mother India, especially Rishikesh, has a history of enchanting and ensnaring me for months at a time, and I usually feel unable to claw my way out back to the rest of the world, in the best way possible.

Reflecting now, I have full-body chills and a leaping heart remembering the exquisite quality of the Himalayan air, the echoing sounds of the temples blaring their mantras over the loudspeakers, and the cold, silent 5 a.m. meditations in the ashram hall with 100 other students.

This time was different. In late February, more news of the virus was on TV every day. I knew it was time to go home. I was also different now. I was no longer a yoga student, roaming backpacker (I once backpacked around the whole of India by train for four months), or young spiritual seeker—I had a serious business to attend to with $60,000 worth of clients embarking on a six-month journey to grow their coaching businesses with me.

We booked a one-way flight to Denpasar and left the next day, my heart breaking to say goodbye to India.

Two weeks later, Bali locked its borders, shut down the airport, and put up one big "closed" sign to tourists for the next two full years.

Tens of thousands of foreigners fled Bali in those weeks, fearing the lack of ventilators and proper healthcare should the pandemic really strike the island hard, but I followed my gut and hunkered down. I felt safe in Bali, and it was ultimately home for both of us.

My biggest fear wasn't getting sick, it was Bali kicking us out at some point and sending us home to our respective countries, where we'd be separated for an unknown amount of time (which happened to friends of ours who didn't serendipitously have the long-term visas we already had).

My other biggest fear was that I was starting my first business mastermind in mid-March 2020, when the entire world was legitimately panicking.

These were the days when almost everywhere was in strict lockdown, toilet paper was sold out on shelves in America, and even the foreigners in Bali were panic-buying groceries and freezing vegetables, afraid the supply chains would dry up and forget about small hippie towns in Indonesia.

Never had I seen something more apocalyptic in my life. None of us had.

I felt as afraid as anyone, with many sleepless nights worrying about everything from "Okay, maybe I am a little scared of this virus after all. Is that a tightness in my chest?" to "What if everyone stops buying anything except food and my new business freezes up, and I'm stranded on an island 8,000 miles away from where I was born?!"

And I knew that people were looking to me for support.

I had amassed a following of a few thousand people online over the previous twelve months and had made almost $100,000 as a coach by this point. I had ten people who were highly invested in this new program who were perhaps thinking about asking for a refund and squirreling away their dollars for the hard winter ahead.

I knew I had to go live again. I knew I had to write. I knew I had to muster up some wisdom and solid business advice for a time like this one.

This was the moment I was truly initiated into the concept of leadership.

To go first.

To come up with the thing to say when no one knows what to say.

Reminiscent of my first ever livestream, I did a little nervous dance around the room before plopping into my desk chair and trying to look like I had it together.

I talked about how the choice to lean into fear or trust exists all the time, and the state of the world was only amplifying it now.

I talked about the ways humans react to the unknown, mostly by anticipating the worst-case scenarios and snowballing their fear, while there's the choice to hold yourself in the unknown with grace and presence: "I don't know what's happening right now or what will happen. And that's okay."

I let them know they weren't alone in their fear and doubt and that I felt it too. I walked them through the process of how I was learning to deal with my own fears by staying in the present moment, remaining grounded in my senses and safety in the immediate environment around me so I could continue to coach my clients, provide support, and take care of myself.

I encouraged those who were in lockdown to see the time as an opportunity and to use it wisely . . . to create. I encouraged them to post, write, share, and offer support to *their* communities. To show up and be a beacon of hope and light. Right now, we need positive thoughts, blind hope, and compassion, I said. We don't need finger pointing that creates division, we need unity around this being a hard time for anyone to know what to do.

I shared that I chose to see it as a prime time for innovation and standing out in the market. Those who continued to show up, serve, and adapt would be the businesses that flourished when this was all over.

There are a lot of things I could have said differently or better, but it worked. It helped.

I did livestreams where people asked me questions about "corona pivots" in their businesses and many wound up choosing that time to invest in learning to get online and rely only on themselves for their income like I was doing. Many of them joined my programs and wound up creating six and multiple-six figures of new income in a new business during one of the most uncertain economic times of our generation.

I posted the following on Instagram in April 2020:

heyelainaray · Follow

heyelainaray What your "new normal" will be depends on what you choose to focus on right now.

Yes, many people have lost their jobs.

Yes, there's a gnarly economic recession happening.

Yes, there's a pandemic of serious proportions occurring.

This does not mean that you just curl up and stop building and stop growing and stop attracting and stop investing.

What would happen to the world if all of us who are in a position to keep serving, creating, and leading just stopped?

Actually, many people have NOT lost their jobs.

Many people are NOT interested in the fear and scarcity and drama and want to make productive use of their time at home.

Many people are experiencing positive life changes.

Many people are healthier than they've ever been.

Many people have more disposable income than they've ever had (no restaurants, bars, shopping, and travel?).

Many people are eager to work on themselves and use this as a growth opportunity.

Every single day I see massive spurts of abundance, well-being, vitality, power, spiritual clarity, and business success for myself, my clients, and those around me.

Because I've chosen to be aware of what's going on AND I keep my mind focused on the best possible outcomes, not the worst.

I am continuing to hold the light for myself and those in my sphere because that's how we're going to get to the other side of all this.

As an entrepreneur, it's so important to watch your mindset and energy.

What are you choosing to focus on right now?"

Not a single member of my new mastermind dropped out or even considered it.

> IT'S EASY TO FEEL GOOD ABOUT BUSINESS WHEN SALES ARE STREAMING IN AND CLIENTS ARE HAPPY AND NUMBERS ARE UP. BUT WHO ARE YOU DURING A MONTH THAT GROSSES $0? WHO ARE YOU WHEN SOMEONE BACKS OUT OF YOUR AGREEMENT? WHO ARE YOU WHEN YOU'RE "DOING ALL THE THINGS" BUT NO NEW SALES CALLS HAVE BEEN BOOKED IN SIX WEEKS?

It seemed my resolution was contagious: to see that time as a launching pad, a time for innovation and planting a leadership stake when other people did freak out, jump ship, and close up shop because they couldn't get grounded enough amongst the chaos. Their people didn't see them as a leader anymore, because during that time, everyone was looking around for someone to listen to who seemed to make sense and who felt good and nourishing to their nervous systems.

I'm proud that I got to be that person for my small community. And not only did my business build a huge amount of trust and momentum and do almost half a million dollars in 2020 (and then a million in 2021), but my clients flourished as well. We navigated one of the weirdest times of our lifetime, together.

We always have the opportunity to succumb to fear in the face of uncertainty, and as entrepreneurs, we face uncertainty on a daily basis. COVID-19 and the pandemic years were an extreme example of this, but by no means does that go away. How do you choose to show up and how do you choose to think about yourself and your business when you're not sure a launch is going to work? Or your tax situation got a little tight unexpectedly and you're not sure if you'll be able to make all your payments next month on time? Or you have an unhappy customer posting nasty things about you on their social media?

Who are you then?

It's easy to feel good about business when sales are streaming in and clients are happy and numbers are up. But who are you during a month that grosses $0? Who are you when someone backs out of your agreement? Who are you when you're "doing all the things" but no new sales calls have been booked in six weeks?

You will be defined by the hard times in your business. You will be defined by the times when it looks like it won't happen or you won't get what you want. These are the times you are tried and tested, when your character is built, and when you as a leader who can *last* is wielded together. This is when your substance is developed, and it is your substance and your beingness that radiates out into the world and creates your match for abundance, clients, influence, and all the other results you desire. It is a match based on your core, and these are the times that define your core.

HOMEWORK FOR THIS CHAPTER

1. What is something you're currently talking about behind closed doors with your close friends or clients that is actually something you should be talking about more publicly in your business? If you're telling your innermost circle and they resonate with it, chances are having that conversation openly will bring in more soul-mate clients.

2. Where do you see yourself anticipating the worst-case scenario in your life or business instead of holding hope or faith? When there's uncertainty at play, can you lean more into the best-case scenario than spiraling into fear?

3. Reflect on your own experience during the pandemic years. How did you have to innovate or adapt your work? What was your biggest lesson that you've taken with you to this day?

CHAPTER 10

GOING ALL IN

LAGOS, NIGERIA
JUNE 23, 2013

There are many things I could attribute my success to, like discipline, hard work, and dumb, blind luck (although I've always said that the harder I work, the luckier I get).

Strategy, learning marketing, and being a good writer and speaker who practices daily also contributed. Consistency pays off and creates a compound effect.

But I know one of the most powerful factors for me growing a business that turned into a million-dollar company in just two years is also the simplest one: I stopped moving around so much.

For seven years before the pandemic, I traveled almost nonstop and didn't own anything that wouldn't fit into two suitcases, one checked, one carry-on.

I once worked for an advertising agency that sent me to live in emerging market countries and produce reports on their economy, with very expensive paid ads featuring certain key government agencies who wanted their pictures in *Time* and *Fortune Magazine*. It was a weird business model, but an epic job to have when you're twenty-five.

I lived in a different country every three months for more than two years.

I had no ties. No boyfriend, no super close friends or family I couldn't live without seeing for a while, and no hometown I felt nostalgic about. Nothing else I'd rather be doing besides seeing the world and getting killer material for my blog. I was a completely free twenty-something pursuing her lifelong dream of being an expat, working for a company that paid for the flights, the housing, the everything—and I got to literally meet the presidents and prime ministers of countries all over the world. I used to want to be a diplomat (hence why I have a degree in Mandarin Chinese), and this was as close as I could get without the stuffy red tape.

One time, I was on assignment in Istanbul for a month when they suddenly called me up and told me I was promoted and going to lead a project in Papua New Guinea. I flew to London to get the visa, only the partner I'd be running the project with got too drunk in Barcelona the night before and didn't make his flight. I was quickly reassigned to the Mongolia project, and the next day was flown to Ulaanbaatar (in winter) in flip-flops and carrying a suitcase packed with clothes for the tropics. I lived there for four months.

We never had any choice in what country we got sent to. If I said no, I was out. I loved the concept, and the adventure.

When I first got hired, I remember thinking that I would honest-to-God go anywhere except Nigeria. That seemed dangerous. Wasn't there a lot of oil and instability due to said oil? Lots of guns there, I mused ignorantly. I had also never been to Africa. Maybe we could start off with somewhere nice and gentle, like Peru or Ireland.

Guess where my first assignment was as a trainee?

Lagos, Nigeria.

I spent three months there, and I probably have permanent damage to my hearing from the sheer volume of life in that city: the car horns blaring, the music blasting, and everyone from the guy hawking puppies at red lights to the parking lot attendants and secretaries at companies we visited needing to YELL AT US TO BE UNDERSTOOD. It just seemed to be how everyone spoke. Loudly!

A cultural curiosity, for sure.

You never walk anywhere in Lagos as a foreigner. You have a driver, and the diplomats have armed drivers. We'd hear about kidnappings on the regular from friends of friends. It was not a joke.

One Sunday, we really wanted to experience a local Christian church where one of our clients was a pastor, but our driver was off for the day. We decided to walk the mere 500 meters from our compound to church and back. On the way home, a guy on a motorbike approached us, saw we were carrying a Bible, and stopped to ask if he could have it. My colleague said yes, amicably, and the guy even gave him a hug before speeding off.

What a strange encounter. Seconds later, my colleague patted down the side of his body and realized his wallet *and* phone were missing.

We were robbed over a Bible. Amazing. I've got to hand it to the guy!

I loved Lagos, though. I partied until 5 a.m. with the locals every weekend, fell head over heels in love with West African music, danced with Femi Kuti on stage on his birthday at the famous Afrika Shrine, and came back to New York calling the Nigerian bouncers at my favorite meatpacking district clubs "oga," to which they'd respond by letting me in VIP every time, wide-eyed laughing and slapping their knees at the tiny blonde girl who somehow knew Nigerian slang. Being well traveled was handy.

I was the woman who could get in a cab in New York, discover the driver was from Egypt, and have an entire conversation in basic Egyptian Arabic. I'd spent a full summer in Cairo when I was nineteen, hitchhiking around doing independent research on the fascinating Chinese diaspora that lived on the outskirts. Yes, that means I speak fluent Mandarin and (at the time) conversational Arabic.

Mexican restaurant? I'd order things that weren't even on the menu after running an entire expansion of the Uber ops team all over Mexico for months without seeing another foreigner. So yes, I'm fluent in Spanish too. Learning languages was a huge part of my life prior to becoming an entrepreneur.

But at some point, I grew weary of being on the road nonstop. The wrinkled clothes. The shampoo exploding in my toiletries bag. The inability to own more than two pairs of earrings or else they'd break in my carry-on. Never mind shoes. I didn't own more than three pairs for five *years*.

And the goodbyes. I had to say goodbye to the nice Welsh guy I started dating in Doha when I lived in Qatar for four months. One day my team called me up and said I was flying to meet the prime minister of Guyana (look that up on the map), and I was off to South America. Then there was the nice Aussie I dated for a few months in Johannesburg before being sent to meet the Omani Minister of Finance in Muscat the next day. Goodbye to the life I had just established for six months in South Africa. The friends from Sweden, Spain, Argentina, and Portugal who I bonded with in such extreme countries and situations and never saw again.

Then there were the years as a backpacker. The cities in Europe where I couldn't afford a taxi to the airport, and I'd have to lug everything I owned on and off the subway, stumbling over myself, drowsy from the flight, yet open-eyed and terrified of being pickpocketed. Crying alone at a train station in Rajasthan after missing a twenty-seven-hour long train ride that took me a week of Indian logistical gymnastics to figure out how to book. Alone. Always alone.

I probably spent close to three years of my life staying in hostel beds that cost less than $25/night. I got bed bugs more times than I can count. I took buses for fifteen hours through the Peruvian Andes and Guatemalan highlands on routes that were notorious for roads collapsing or buses merely running off the side of a cliff.

At some point, it became apparent that I needed and wanted to settle down. Travel had irreversibly changed my life for the better. Sixty countries later, most of them places the average American could neither pronounce nor place on a map, I was truly a world citizen, far removed from the ordinary world of busing tables at a pizzeria and saving up a thousand dollars to stake my claim at freedom beyond the Buffalo suburbs.

But it had become a bit pathological. What was I running from? Was I a lost soul after all?

My dad, bless his heart, kept a giant map of the world in the basement of our house. There, he marked each place I traveled with a little red thumbtack. Every time I went somewhere new, he faithfully looked it up, raised his eyebrows, said a prayer, and stuck in another pin until the world looked like it had chicken pox.

Only now do I know, after years of healing and therapy, that I was indeed running back then.

I wasn't capable of long-term intimacy or commitment with the ordinary world. Beginning from my days of hyper-achievement in high school that ended my history of being bullied, I consistently learned to settle for the *admiration* from others for being the girl who traveled the farthest instead of seeking *love* from someone who could hold me the closest.

It wasn't even when I moved to Bali that I settled down, it was when I met my beloved and got to experience what real love and companionship felt like that my entire body and mind relaxed. A nervous system that had been running around the world for close to a decade rebooted and came online in a healthier way.

René's love, Mama Bali's enduring pull on my heartstrings, and the coronavirus pandemic created a cocktail that would have me stay in one house, in one country, on one island, with one man, with one group of friends for two years, uninterrupted.

As the borders closed and it became apparent that I wouldn't be going anywhere for a while, I feared being ordinary without the Instagram pictures of me riding horses in Mongolia, sleeping among the Omo Valley tribes in Ethiopia, and shaking hands with the president of Paraguay. Who was I without the wild travel stories?

It turns out that I was a pretty good businesswoman and coach.

It turns out that I was more than halfway decent with money, once I had some.

It turns out that I was a really good girlfriend to the first boyfriend I had in my adult life.

And it turns out that I actually have a side of me that likes being at home with my cats!

That place where I was planting roots wasn't anything like I had expected to have at age thirty. I thought I'd be back in New York or California, but it was precisely the opposite side of the planet that felt best to me. Maybe my astrological chart read better when turned upside down and my soul figured it out first?

My bank account liked all of this as much as my heart did.

A long-term visa, a long-term partner, and a long-term vision for my career as an entrepreneur were all *groundbreaking* things for me to have in the spring of 2020.

Free of the part-time gigs and free of the temptation to do things like motorbike around Vietnam again, I directed my focus completely onto my business. I poured the energy and passion I had for movement and adventure into my work.

I chose growing my business to be my next big adventure, and it responded by showering me with clients, inquiries, and true financial abundance. Private clients were paying me $10,000 pay-in-fulls, and for the first time in my life, I saw my checking account balance hit nearly six figures in cash.

Looks like the piece I had been missing all along was simply . . . stability.

Focus.

Home.

These healthy masculine energies provided a container for my feminine energies of creativity and passion to flow and be appropriately developed.

One of the biggest ways I see my clients or people in my personal life sabotage the true nature of the work they are meant to create at the true level of bigness they are meant to create it at is by continuously hopping around from thing to thing, place to place, and idea to idea without properly allowing time and commitment to cultivate the results that are possible from those things, places, and ideas.

When clients are evaluating whether they want to work with you, one of the things they will subconsciously pick up on is if you are a safe place for them to invest their money. Are you stable? Committed? Professional? Focused? Are you setting an example with your lifestyle, even well outside the scope of what they are hiring you for, that they feel a resonance with and an aspiration to mirror some aspects of that themselves?

Or are you barely holding it together, hopping around from home to home or country to country, launching something and then having three months off-line, posting religiously for a month and then getting disheartened with the results and going rogue for another month?

ONE OF THE BIGGEST WAYS I SEE MY CLIENTS OR PEOPLE IN MY PERSONAL LIFE SABOTAGE THE TRUE NATURE OF THE WORK THEY ARE MEANT TO CREATE AT THE TRUE LEVEL OF BIGNESS THEY ARE MEANT TO CREATE IT AT IS BY CONTINUOUSLY HOPPING AROUND FROM THING TO THING, PLACE TO PLACE, AND IDEA TO IDEA WITHOUT PROPERLY ALLOWING TIME AND COMMITMENT TO CULTIVATE THE RESULTS THAT ARE POSSIBLE FROM THOSE THINGS, PLACES, AND IDEAS.

Money is attracted to stable energy. Clients are attracted to consistency. It feels safe. And one of the biggest actions I took to call in more money and more clients more consistently was committing to one home, one business idea, one man, and one direction, then really giving it my all.

Exercise: Sometimes clients will come to me and ask, "Elaina, I have a really bad pattern around inconsistency" or "I have this money wound where I spend uncontrollably and get myself into a bad spot with my finances. How do I fix it?"

Here's my quintessential, cover-all answer for any "how do I fix this thing I have going on that I don't want to have going on" type questions: You don't fix it.

Listen carefully. You don't fix it. Don't focus on what you don't want, focus on what you do want. Watch your well-intentioned desire to fix, psychoanalyze, heal, understand, and process *the wound* instead of focusing on the alternative state of being, thoughts, behaviors, feelings, and actions that are available for you to step in to as a practice and can generate big results (especially when accompanied by depth work, healing, inner mastery, and the like). Realize that you're not broken and there's nothing to fix, there's just where you desire to go and how you choose to show up for those desires. Where you've been, while it is valuable and contributes to who you are today, is still not as paramount as where you desire to be and your determination to become that version of yourself. Choose that available timeline of reality.

You also don't fixate on "fixing it" before you do the things you're called to do and know you're meant to be doing. You feel your way through it, yes. But you also continue to move forward, one powerful step at a time. You feel it to heal it and move with it while still pursuing your goals and visions and taking action on things you need to. You do not give energy to overanalyzing this pattern or wound or unsavory habit of yours, which may continue to keep you stuck rather than moving forward and healing the pattern through new actions, new feedback, and new evidence, all which can reinforce new beliefs and create a stronger and more up-to-date self-concept.

Continuously shift your focus to what you do want and how you do want to be and feel. Practice it daily. So, instead of doing years of energy healing on your inconsistency and reading trauma books trying to understand that this comes from when you were three years old and your mom became a single mom and started working so her presence in your life became more inconsistent and then you've replicated that pattern into adulthood . . . you could simply focus on how you can get into the energy and habit of being consistent today.

What actions can you take now to be consistent? How can you get accountable to this new way of being you're going to practice more often now? How can you take one simple step each day toward embodying the final result, the new identity, the new way of being that you're desiring? This is how you reinforce a new way of being that's available to you now.

DON'T FOCUS ON WHAT YOU DON'T WANT, FOCUS ON WHAT YOU DO WANT. WATCH YOUR WELL-INTENTIONED DESIRE TO FIX, PSYCHOANALYZE, HEAL, UNDERSTAND, AND PROCESS THE WOUND INSTEAD OF FOCUSING ON THE ALTERNATIVE STATE OF BEING, THOUGHTS, BEHAVIORS, FEELINGS, AND ACTIONS THAT ARE AVAILABLE FOR YOU TO STEP IN TO AS A PRACTICE AND CAN GENERATE BIG RESULTS.

HOMEWORK FOR THIS CHAPTER

1. In which areas of your life do you need to stabilize and create more of a container for yourself? Pick one and create a clean-up plan that you can start today.

2. Moving around a lot was my biggest self-sabotaging pattern. What is yours? Then don't focus on fixing it, focus on cementing the opposite, desired result that you do want to have. How can you instill one new action or behavior from today forward that will counteract this old tendency? (That's all it is: a tendency. And you're powerful enough to become aware of it and create a new one.)

3. Where are you *still* trying to analyze, fix, and figure out some "undesirable" quality of yours? Instead, imagine yourself going around and living life fully embodied in the opposite and desired quality you would like to move into. How does this version of you show up in the world? How do you make decisions as this person? What do you do every morning that's different? How do you create differently in the business? Find three easy ways to be more like that version of yourself today.

CHAPTER 11

MAKING EXPANSIVE FINANCIAL DECISIONS AND WIELDING YOUR ECONOMIC POWER

UBUD, BALI, INDONESIA
AUGUST 15, 2020

One of the most important lessons I've learned as a business owner is that there's a never-ending series of identity shifts you go through in order to do your job adequately.

And a never-ending series of blind flying leaps into dark, rugged terrain to get there.

Because who you see yourself as is one of the biggest determining factors in what you wind up accomplishing.

For the first three decades of my life, I didn't see myself as an entrepreneur, and I had to slowly ease myself into that identity like I'd lower myself into a steaming hot bath: with slight trepidation. Once I sighed and stretched my toes into the warm waters of being a real business owner and felt like I really belonged there, my business became more and more successful.

In the same way, I never saw myself as an investor in real estate or homeowner.

Up until recently, I believed that someday I would "settle down" and buy a house back in the United States and let my passport mold in a desk drawer. I'd have domesticated indoor American cats instead of my girls here in Bali who come from a long lineage of wild, ruthless felines who decapitate geckos and chase pretty tropical birds for fun. Instead, I'd go on Target runs and get Amazon delivered to an actual address. Maybe I'd drive a four-wheeler instead of my island scooter.

All these ideas shifted in an instant when I walked into my villa in Ubud.

As the uncertainty of riding out a pandemic in a foreign country increased, René proposed that we move in together. I had started to feel less safe living alone in the moldy bungalow while an island whose men depend on tourism for work were suddenly restless and empty-pocketed. Crime, regrettably, had gone up temporarily in Bali, and everyone's nervous systems were pretty shot from the first two months of the pandemic.

We spent a few months looking at villas, which all would normally be full of tourists paying $100 to $500/night. No owner would ever do long-term leasing in regular times.

But the real estate market had been brought to its knees overnight, and we had a unique opportunity to find an unusually incredible first home together. We figured we'd lease it for six months, then the high-paying tourists would come back, and we'd be kicked out.

Walking through the enormous wooden door to my now-home changed everything.

It was love at first sight.

First of all, the place looks like a bona fide retreat center. It has four bedrooms, which is perfect for each of us to have a separate bedroom and office. The winding path through a huge garden leads to a fully enclosed living room and kitchen (rare in Bali), with floor-to-ceiling glass windows, high ceilings with wooden beams, and a modern, open-floor plan designed to perfection in what I would call "Balifornia" minimalist style. A large Buddha statue is the focal point of the living area, one of my favorite elements of the house.

But the absolute signature feature is an actual Olympic-sized swimming pool running the length of the property, dotted by four perfect white umbrellas and sunbeds. The villa is enclosed by four tall white walls on all sides of the property so there's total privacy and quiet from the neighboring family villas in a very desirable area pleasantly outside of Ubud.

We had to have it.

It was four times as much as I've paid for rent anywhere in my entire life, and we negotiated nonstop for days before we signed a one-year lease, the only option the owners would entertain. It was brand new, like literally only days old.

> YOU'RE WORTHY. YOU'RE ALLOWED TO TAKE UP SPACE. YOU'RE ALLOWED TO HAVE SOMETHING REALLY NICE. YOU'RE SAFE. SET DOWN YOUR BAGS AND LAY YOUR WEARY HEAD HERE.

Shortly after moving in, I knew I would never be able to leave.

The emotional upgrades were huge and instantaneous. After living in hostel beds for years, settling for one-room bungalows, and making do with a huge variety of hygiene standards all around the world, I finally got to tell myself: You're worthy. You're allowed to take up space. You're allowed to have something *really* nice. You're safe. Set down your bags and lay your weary head here.

I had been surviving for so long, the instinct buried deep in my DNA from Irish and Italian ancestors who legitimately had to escape persecution and poverty by leaving their homes.

I had never prioritized my home and living environment in my entire life. I grew up in a home so tiny that I couldn't have childhood sleepovers. We never hosted the holidays. If my parents had guests over, they moved the kitchen table into the living room and squeezed an extra two chairs between the couches.

I lived in a dorm room all four years of college. Even when I moved to New York, I shared a room in the East Village for the first year to save money on rent so I could save up to go traveling again.

With this house, though, I assumed the identity of a thirty-year-old woman who had *made it*. Who lived in the home of her dreams in her favorite place in the world and did what she loved for a living.

The villa also made me feel alive and inspired.

Waking up in a gorgeous home made it easy to write. I channeled a new program almost instantly. I hired a new business coach and made $100,000 in six weeks, an absolute mind-boggling new record in my business. I felt amazing, taken care of, supported, and abundant.

Living with René also added a new dynamic to my life: being in true partnership. I had support. I had someone to go grocery shopping with and put my carrots and almond milk next to in the fridge. I had someone I loved waking up next to and sneaking into bed with, someone (a man!) who knew what to do when the power went out.

It was his idea, shortly after moving in, that I buy the place.

BUY IT?! I looked at him with crazy marsupial eyes, sputtering out my celery juice. I had made less than $200,000 in my own business at that point, and I was sure the place cost a lot more than that. There were no friendly mortgages offered to foreigners buying villas in Bali.

Was it even for sale?

> I KNEW MYSELF TO BE SOMEONE WHO MOVED FAST, HOPPED ON OPPORTUNITIES THAT FELT RIGHT, AND WALKED OUT ONTO THE LEDGE, OVER AND OVER AGAIN. I HAD FOLLOWED MY INTUITION AROUND THE WORLD AND BACK AGAIN, AND IT HADN'T FAILED ME YET.

Days later, I was on the phone with a very shocked (and stern) Italian woman. She couldn't believe a bright young woman wanted to buy her place in this time of complete economic chaos.

And she was no-nonsense. She gave me a number, the only number, and I could take it or leave it. The place was brand new, precious to her, and she was confident the market would eventually turn around.

The number made me feel dizzy. Irresponsible.

Thankfully, René already owned a home in the Netherlands and knew how this all worked, and he believed it was a solid investment and a smart, yet bold move. I believed him, wobbling into home ownership like a baby walking for the first time.

I asked, sheepishly but earnestly, for a little . . . payment plan.

And this was how it came to be that I bought a luxury villa in a foreign country two months into a global pandemic and huge economic recession. Before I knew it, notaries were coming to our new house, and I was sticking my thumbs into ink, signing away my life in Indonesian.

Buying my first home was another enormous emotional upgrade. It was terrifying.

I was yet again doing something I didn't believe myself capable of doing. I was taking a huge, flying leap off a cliff with no safe landing in sight. I thought that perhaps I'd own a home in my, you know, forties? I had just come from vagabonding around the world for seven years. I simply didn't see myself as a homeowner. I didn't understand real estate, no less in Bali. I didn't understand how I'd even take care of the place or how I'd renegotiate the land contract or pay taxes or make sure I didn't get screwed over in the hundreds of possible ways I was opening myself up to being screwed. Was I ready for this step? While living with a boyfriend who I'd only been dating for less than a year?

No. I was not "ready."

Yet I knew this was who I knew myself to be. I knew myself to be someone who moved fast, hopped on opportunities that felt right, and walked out onto the ledge, over and over again. I had followed my intuition around the world and back again, and it hadn't failed me yet.

So, I leapt.

I stepped into being the version of myself who was already a savvy international real estate investor.

And the resources presented themselves.

The owners softened to me immediately upon getting large sums of cold hard cash transferred to their accounts and seeing my signature in ink. I was for real.

They flew out to Bali as soon as they could, and we started to get to know each other. They took us out for dinner, and we had them over

> YOU DESIRE SOMETHING. YOU DECIDE. YOU FLING YOURSELF OFF A CLIFF. THEN THE ANSWERS COME.

to the newly redecorated house where they seemed to look a little painfully at each other with realization that it wasn't theirs anymore. As it turns out, they own hundreds of properties all around the world and are mega real estate experts. They took both of us under their wing.

René started to learn the ropes, and he purchased another piece of land where he has now built three villas. I bought another piece of land next door and built an extension on the villa the following year. All the questions and doubts I had were answered by people who I knew and trusted and who suddenly appeared to show me the way—after I said yes.

This is how it works, my friends.

You desire something. You decide. You fling yourself off a cliff. Then the answers come.

One of the biggest common mistakes aspiring entrepreneurs who never get off the ground make is that they wait. They do research, wanting to feel prepared and ready. They want to be responsible and get it right.

But these well-meaning and rational humans may never become wildly successful business owners because they are missing *the whole point.*

THERE IS NO READY. THERE IS NOTHING THAT CAN PREPARE YOU FOR THE UTTER MINEFIELD OF TAKING OWNERSHIP OF SOMETHING YOU'VE NEVER DONE BEFORE.

THE KEY IS TO TAKE THE FIRST FIVE STEPS, RUNNING, AND THEN FIGURE IT OUT AS YOU GO.

There is no ready. There is nothing that can prepare you for the utter minefield of taking ownership of something you've never done before.

The key is to take the first five steps, running, and then figure it out as you go.

I wrote a post on Facebook in March 2022, about six weeks out from finishing the entire investment:

> **Elaina Ray** is at **Bali, Indonesia. Island of Gods.**
> 17 March · Badung, Indonesia
>
> "This might actually break me."
>
> Literal words I said to myself for months after deciding to buy my dream villa in Bali two months into the pandemic.
>
> **People had fled the country. Investors had backed out.** Properties were being abandoned. The airport was shut down, borders were closed, toilet paper was sold out worldwide. We were all having the weirdest moment in collective human history.
>
> This was no time to like, buy a luxury home. In a foreign country.
>
> But I was being guided. I was led to the door, and when I walked through, there was no going back. (You know those moments in your own life, right?) I couldn't NOT live there and have it.

But the tiny issue was that it cost more than all the money that I had ever earned in my still-stabilizing business up until that point . . . and then some.

So naturally, I said yes. (After definitely some sleepless nights and deep self-reckoning.) But I trusted myself. I trusted my yes. And I rose to the occasion.

In the months after this "reckless" purchase, my business virtually doubled. I paid every payment on time, in full.

Fast-forward a year after that, still in a pandemic, still no tourists, still a fully weird time, and I was guided to buy the land next door to the house AND to say yes to a massive extension on the property that was valued at even more than the original villa was.

I thought, "Okay, I'm making good money now, but this might be taking it too far; this might actually break me. I mean, I still need to pay US taxes and be a responsible business owner. This is really pushing it."

But I said yes again. I leaned in.

Today, we are about six weeks from finishing the entire project, and I'm just a month or two away from the final payment on the payment plan for the entire crazy-ass project.

It's been a breakthrough moment, for sure.

Whenever you say yes to something big and scary and so meant for you, it's a portal. A portal to your power, to knowing what you're truly capable of, of seeing the big dream outside of you that you see inside of you right now.

It doesn't mean it's easy and you feel the certainty right away. **Sometimes you just need to say yes, and the feeling finds you** later on the other side.

In the meantime, you trust. You have faith. You choose to back yourself because you know what you're made of.

I know I'm made of the material who always honors her money commitments, who makes smart, bold investments, who acts in exactly the right timing, who is constantly elevating.

And going forward with this big, crazy dream reinforced that identity and self-knowing, and I've come out even stronger.

What do you need to say yes to today? Especially to something you're not sure you can pull off?

The activation lies therein—AFTER you say yes. On the other side.

So leap.

One of the biggest things I've learned about money is that money loves a purpose. It loves knowing where it's going and having intention behind its use. I've never made more money than in the months when I was really clear on a big, expansive new something or other I wanted to get, whether it was my house or a new team member or a new handbag I had my eye on. Money came easily right into my stewardship, and it went right out into the thing I desired. After deciding to buy my Bali home, my income skyrocketed because I had such a clear motivation and destination for the new money to go. Money in, money out. I've also never made more money than in the months when I was releasing money liberally and intentionally (but not carelessly spending by any means). When there was a lot of flow moving through my financial channel, it seemed that the channel for receiving expanded and more resources came in because of the healthy movement.

Here's what I want you to do. You're going to do a little financial planning experiment with me. I've done the exercise in the months when I've brought in the most revenue (which, at the time of this writing is $192,800 cash in one month, and we're going to double that this year).

Decide exactly how much revenue you want to bring in this month. Pick a number that feels juicy and stretchy and exciting. Then ask yourself, "What am I going to do with this money?" and create a detailed plan for exactly where the money is going to go. Don't worry about where the money will come from, just play along in this little experiment with me and, just for this month, focus on the energy of where it's going out and what you're going to receive when you have this amount of money. Make sure you've picked "destinations" for the money that feel exciting and connected to your heart, not simply paying the bills or ordinary expenses. You must include items that you're expanding your income and receiving ability in order to have.

One of the biggest things I catch my clients doing that cripples their financial flow and potential is really obsessing about calculating where the money they say they want in a month is going to *come from*. Scribbling numbers in their journals like "Okay, to hit $15K this month, I need to get 3 private clients at $1,500/month plus 10 group coaching clients at $500/month plus . . ." and until the numbers add up, they can't get behind the number. It's not that I don't think about the possible avenues for earning in every month, but what I focus on instead is where I'm going and what resources I need to go there and what I'm meant to create. I know I have a choice to just decide my desired level of income and, as much as I'm tempted, I can't predict where each dollar will come from. Trying to do so puts a proverbial dollar sign on the head of each potential client, as I can't help but see where they might plug into my financial jigsaw puzzle. I've done it that way in the past and let me tell

> you that a) it didn't generate the results I wanted for the month, and b) it felt icky. I lost sight of my creative genius and the people on the other end of each purchase coming into the business.
>
> Deciding to focus on where the money is *going* instead of where the money is *coming from*, and focusing on widening my financial channel intentionally through smart investment, expansive identity work, and feel-good business decisions that create more opportunities for people to come into my world and fall in love with what I do over the long term, is what helped me reach my financial goals the most.

I've found that having a business structure where you have a diversified product suite and several different ways for people to work with you is beneficial and offers many practical channels for money to come in. In my business, I have free content, low-cost masterclasses, self-study digital courses for a few thousand dollars, high-ticket masterminds (and multiple levels to serve different clients' needs), and private coaching. I can relax into knowing that as long as I continue to actively sell what I'm called to sell, put my work out there, write, speak, and teach what I'm meant to teach, and be a visible person on the internet, people will come in and plug into my work at the level of support and investment that's appropriate for them. This allows me not to micromanage where the six- or multiple-six-figures cash that we reliably bring into the business each month (today) comes from, and instead focus on operating in my zone of genius: being the CEO behind an epic personal brand and living my best life while doing it.

On another note about investing, you're never too early to start investing and developing your knowledge around how to wield economic influence and resources. Personally, I like working in percentages instead of fixed dollar amounts for saving and investing purposes. This suits entrepreneurs because your income inevitably fluctuates, but no matter how much you earn, you can always siphon off 10 percent here or there for each of your investment buckets. One of the biggest mistakes you can make is thinking that you will do those things when you have more money, when the truth is you actually need to have intentional systems around your personal finances first *before* more money can flow in. By being a good steward of the money you do already have, you are likely to attract more of it and know what to do with it when it does come.

Here's how I currently do things. I have my accountant track all my business and personal expenses in two separate P&L (profit and loss) documents so I have insight into both areas of my financial world. Every month I sit down and have "deep dive" time in my money (studies show the more time you spend on your money management, the more money you'll have[5]). I take the amount of cash received that month (I don't care about sales made, just cash that has actually come in) and subtract my expenses and taxes for the month. Of the remaining amount, I pay my personal expenses and set aside a bit extra for fun and spending. Then I put 10 percent of the remainder into long-term savings, 10 percent into other investment buckets (maybe that month it's cryptocurrency, maybe it's my SEP IRA and retirement accounts—I just tune into where I want it to go that month), 10 percent into real estate, and 10 percent into further reinvestment in myself or the business, which could be mentorship, retreats, courses, i.e., whatever supports my personal and professional development as the head of the business. Then anything left over goes into my personal fun and enjoyment account.

> YOU ACTUALLY NEED TO HAVE INTENTIONAL SYSTEMS AROUND YOUR PERSONAL FINANCES FIRST BEFORE MORE MONEY CAN FLOW IN. BY BEING A GOOD STEWARD OF THE MONEY YOU DO ALREADY HAVE, YOU ARE LIKELY TO ATTRACT MORE OF IT AND KNOW WHAT TO DO WITH IT WHEN IT DOES COME.

It is not a perfect system, and it's not one you need to exactly replicate as much as use as inspiration for finding your own way of doing things. You might have a travel fund instead of a real estate account or an angel investor fund instead of cryptocurrency. The point is to start now, use percentages so that you're always able to set money aside for the future even if you have a dip in revenue, and set aside money for your tax bill ahead of time so you don't have any unexpected surprises, which can happen to entrepreneurs who aren't yet familiar with self-employment and corporate taxation. It's never too early to hire an accountant and financial adviser and have things well structured from the beginning. It means you're building on a solid foundation.

HOMEWORK FOR THIS CHAPTER

1. Identity shifting exercise. Where do you feel like an impostor with how you're handling your finances right now? Where are you worried that you're going to mess up or get it wrong? Where do you think you're "not there yet" or that someone else would know how to do it better than you? Now, can you counteract each of those unhelpful stories and decide that you're completely smart, capable, and effective and are already learning everything you need to learn in order to be an economic powerhouse and wield your financial resources like the boss you already are? (Nobody knows how to invest or make these decisions until they simply start and learn as they go. You will get better over time, you just have to start. Don't feel like you're supposed to have it all figured out beforehand.)

2. Consider hiring a financial adviser. Even if you are only making $1,000 per month and you set up a system to set aside $50 into a few investment buckets, you will be showing money and the universe that you are ready for more. Having a solid management system in place, regardless of your current income, sets you up to make better financial decisions long term.

3. What is one area you're really wanting to invest in when you think of yourself two to five years from now? How could you start to do that right now, even if it means doing it on a super small scale or setting aside small increments of money every month with the intention of it going into that final destination that really excites you?

4. Money and creativity respond to your energy, and your energy is impacted by your environment. For me, getting my dream villa was a huge upgrade to my business because I felt so abundant, inspired, and supported in my new home, and I became more magnetic as a result (and more productive). You don't have to buy a new house to feel this way. Take a look at your living space and make some upgrades. **Where could you make a space where you feel inspired to create magnificence?** Where might just adding a piece of art, a few candles, or an extra plant really make a difference? Might investing in a housekeeper to come once a week free up your time and improve how you feel in your space? Decide on three little home improvements to make, do them this week, and notice how you feel.

CHAPTER 12

THE FEMININE ENERGY INITIATION AND BUILDING MY DREAM TEAM

UBUD, BALI, INDONESIA
JUNE 9, 2020

While I don't believe any sacrifice is required when you start earning more money, the truth is that if you're not prepared or it happens so fast that you didn't see it coming, the increased client flow after a big explosion in business can cause chaos to take the reins.

This scenario is precisely what happened after I signed for my dream home and my business started to take off toward the half-million-dollar mark. I was poorly prepared on the infrastructure side of the business when it came to managing this volume of sales.

I remember sitting down to dinner one night that my boyfriend had lovingly prepared because I had been too busy on calls all day to eat, only to realize, *shit shit shit, I have another evening call with a private client in New York*. I wolfed down a few bites, then flew back to my office, leaving the plate half full with food and him angrily cleaning up the dishes.

Time zones were a bitch. Having no boundaries was also a bitch.

There were a few months like that.

I had clients crawling out of my ears from a new group program, the mastermind I launched at the start of the pandemic, and a roster full of private clients. Everyone seemed needy to me, and they were driving me nuts. It was around this time that I had my first client-from-hell experience, which I endured because I wasn't confident enough to set 'em loose like I would be now. I was a people pleaser. I answered dozens of questions in the Facebook groups for all my programs, caretaking everybody's emotions.

I was making more money than ever, but I wasn't choosing the highest timeline for how those results could *feel*. I was exhausted and resentful. Something had to shift, and fast. Otherwise, I knew I was going to push away the one man who really loved me, and I'd wind up single and burned out.

The first thing I did was redo my entire calendar. I established that I was only working from 10 a.m. to 5 p.m. Bali time, and anyone who didn't like that or couldn't work around my availability shouldn't hire me. I had to be willing to risk losing clients to save my sanity.

Then I started hiring. I only had one virtual assistant at that point, and she was wonderful. She posted all my writing on social media, she engaged with new followers, and she handled some of the basic administration of calendaring clients and managing the web developer.

I knew I needed someone who could be my "energetic bouncer," who could help me run the business from a logistical and operational point of view, manage my clients in a more hands-on way, and create a buffer between me and the mobs of people who felt like blood-hungry zombies with their eyes on my jugular. I wanted to be able to play more in my zone of genius: teaching, writing, and coaching, and less on managing the day-to-day "where's the link to the replay of yesterday's training?" (which we *just* sent out) sort of questions that made me want to drive my scooter off a ledge into the Indonesian jungle.

A Chief Operations Officer, I mused. *But where would I find one? That was a big-girl hire.*

I worked with my coach at the time to draft up the job description, sent it out in exactly one email, and the first person to respond was Hannah.

And I hired her the same way I've hired everyone from my podcast manager to our present-day support coaches to the publishing agency who helped me get this very book into your hands.

I look at the name of the person, and I know.

It's literally some kind of energetic signature on their name, and it's a gut reaction, a soul-knowing yes or no.

I have to pay attention or I miss it, but I've never second-guessed the wisdom in hiring the immediate my-soul-says-yes person.

Next, I needed a support coach. I needed someone else who knew her stuff, shared my business philosophy, and had a complementary skill set to mine, like copywriting or mindset coaching. I followed my little process, made one post on social media, and Lauren came right in out of left field. I knew she was the one, although I was admittedly a little intimidated because she was *the* copywriter of our time and industry and had worked for some big-name coaches I admired. She wanted to work with me?!

Over the course of just a few weeks, I went from an overworked, one-woman show with a VA and a part-time web developer to effectively a CEO, with a lead operations manager with two decades of marketing experience, the best copywriter in our industry as my support coach, an upgraded social media manager, and my web developer who built my first website and still works for us. Today, I've added in another two support coaches (and Lauren's moved on to rightfully dominate in her own company), a podcast manager, a sales lead, a marketing assistant, and a whole bona fide social media agency.

Building out my team was a dream come true and a really smooth process, to be honest. I couldn't believe I was making enough money to pay other people well enough to work for me . . . ahem, I mean *us*, and to take it as seriously as I do. Some people want to believe that hiring has to be a long, hard, complicated, and expensive process, and that's simply 100 percent optional. Hiring, for me, has always been straightforward. I trust myself, and I trust the person. *I have to.*

After a roughly six-week hiring spree, I was finally able to slow down. Lauren took calls with my clients and started teaching the details of copywriting and messaging that had been making me pound my head against my desk after every call in which I repeated myself for the fifteenth time. Hannah protected my calendar like it was the last freshwater source on earth and handled all client communications.

Finally, I was held. I viscerally understood what it meant to be supported, to be able to lean on and trust others in the same way I was learning to lean on and trust my partner ten months into our relationship.

I had to trust my team. The whole circus had gotten too big. This was far beyond doing it all by myself anymore.

Most importantly, I vowed not to launch any new offers for a while and focus on scaling the programs I already had, therefore simplifying my product suite and allowing time to scale and integrate the new team. I had actually sold two seats in the second round of my signature program for brand-new coaches, and I did something I've only done once in my career: I apologized, told them the program no longer existed, and gave them both refunds. One hated my guts and probably still does, and the other joined a different program later and wound up landing an $80,000 client.

I burned the damn thing down. Sometimes you have to.

And I swore off privately coaching or running group programs for brand-spanking-new coaches. I realized that my zone of genius was not trying to convince someone that it was okay to charge for their services or coach them on the fear of being visible on social media. I had surpassed those obstacles long ago, and as it works in an industry like this, the business had to keep up with my evolution. I was ready for higher-level clients, higher-level problems to solve, and more of my own unique creativity to come out to bat.

The near burnout had come because I was not only not supported, but because I was also not being true to my next level. I was underestimating myself, serving clients aligned to a previous version of myself, and selling myself short on exploring another level of my expertise as a coach that would make me feel excited again.

The radical changes worked.

By the end of the hiring process and my thirty-first birthday, I hit my first six-figure month with smoke from the smoldering pile of my old business still hanging in the air. Yes, you read that correctly. September 2020 was a $100,000 cash *month,* which is like the holy grail in the coaching industry. More on that shortly.

First, here's what I want you to know about hiring. Number one, it's never too soon to have support. You don't have to get to some preapproved, preordained stage of business before you're allowed to have a VA or a social media manager or whatever type of help you want. There's no reason why you can't right here and right now hire a VA who works five hours per week for you and takes some of the day-to-day administrative tasks off your plate, lets you practice the art of delegating, and gets you into the vibe of being a team leader in addition to owner of the business.

Some of my clients hire a team before they make a single dollar in their business. For some, it feels best to have support from the beginning to get the thing off the ground. Others grow their businesses to well over seven figures completely on their own and then hire a team. The key here is not following any kind of formula but rather tuning into what you want and creating a business based on that.

Present day, I have eight members on my team. I know, that sounds like a lot, but I promise you I hired them one at a time, one step at a time. Here's the breakdown of who works for me and a little bit of what they do, just to give you some inspiration.

CHIEF OPERATIONS OFFICER/LEAD SUPPORT COACH: She basically runs the business behind the scenes so I can just coach, create content, and be the visionary of the business. She onboards clients, manages all the clients and other team members, does tracking and reporting on the business, manages my calendar, does sales calls, and is the lead support coach to help our clients with operations, backend systems, SOPs, and hiring. Essentially, she makes sure all I have to do is say, "I want to sell xyz next month," and she's on it, making sure everyone else on the team gets their part in that lined up, plus comes up with ideas to improve the overall business structure and efficiency.

CHIEF TECHNOLOGY OFFICER: He handles everything to do with my website, all our sales pages and opt-ins, integrations, payment portals, backend automations, funnels, the membership site where I house all our trainings and courses for clients, plus does company troubleshooting of all kinds. He also edits videos, does incredible design work, and is a general saint.

CREATIVE DIRECTOR/SOCIAL MEDIA SUPPORT COACH: She is in charge of repurposing content from the backend vault of all the things I've ever written and said on video, getting those things onto Instagram, Facebook, and email. She manages my Facebook group and our paid ads, maintains my Pinterest and blog presence, and supervises our graphic designer who creates beautiful imagery for all our programs and promos. Her agency does my Instagram engagement, books me on podcasts and summits for additional visibility, and implements audience growth strategies. She also personally coaches my mastermind clients on social media strategy.

MARKETING MANAGER: She works with me to oversee the agency and our social media marketing activities. She makes sure the sales plan aligns with what the agency is putting out, double-checks that people are aware of all our products and services, drives sales to "secondary products" (like our many masterclasses, low-end products, and self-study courses), updates automations, figures out what's converting best, comes up with creative new sales and marketing ideas, and is a general jack-of-all-trades.

PODCAST MANAGER: I simply record the audio conversations with the podcast guests and send them to her and she completely edits and produces the episodes, creates all promotional materials for each episode, and manages our iTunes and Spotify presence. (Look for *Million Dollar Spirit Business* and subscribe so you don't miss our new releases.)

COPYWRITING SUPPORT COACH: She's a genius. She looks at our clients' social media content, teaches them messaging and marketing skills that will eventually make them millions of dollars, and handles the nitty-gritty of being in their copy with them while teaching the nuance behind being persuasive and authentic online.

MINDSET SUPPORT COACH: Our mindset coach is trauma certified and runs breakout sessions for our mastermind clients so they have somewhere safe to go when emotions run high and they become overwhelmed or discouraged during the business growth journey. I am, however, clear with my clients that triggers, childhood wounds, and recurring emotional patterns are not our zone of genius as a company and that they should always be working with a certified psychotherapist alongside their work on growing the business.

SALES LEAD: She handles my sales calls for the Sapphire and Diamond masterminds. She's been through most of my programs herself and loves our work, so it makes it easy for her to talk naturally about what we offer. Not to mention, I've personally trained her in sales, so she rocks at it.

> CONTRARY TO POPULAR BELIEF, THE UNCOMFORTABLE TRUTH IS THAT BRINGING SOMEONE ONTO YOUR TEAM USUALLY CAUSES A TEMPORARY INCREASE IN YOUR TIME, MONEY, AND ENERGY INVESTMENT, FOLLOWED BY BIG, LONG-TERM PAYOFFS ONCE THEY ARE WELL INTEGRATED INTO THE BUSINESS.

Know that one of the biggest mistakes I help my clients avoid is thinking that hiring an online business manager (OBM) or a social media agency is going to fix all their problems and that it will instantly reduce their workload and make their life easier.

Contrary to popular belief, the uncomfortable truth is that bringing someone onto your team usually causes a temporary increase in your time, money, and energy investment, followed by big, long-term payoffs once they are well integrated into the business. If you want to set this person up to succeed, you're going to need to onboard them correctly, set up clear guidelines and expectations for the role, communicate regularly with them, and train them in the way you work and how you want things done. There's a natural learning curve to this process. If you don't anticipate it, you'll think something is wrong with you, or you'll be unreasonably critical of new hires when everything doesn't click into place in thirty days with minimal oversight on your part.

Most everyone has been on my team at this point for close to two years, and we continue growing together year after year. The investment I've put into my working relationship with each person has paid off many times over. As a result, I'm able to work almost exclusively in my zone of genius and for just a few hours per day. But what actually happens is that there's not just a mere reduction of working hours for you as the CEO, but there's also a shift in the nature of the work you're doing. You move from heavy lifting a wide range of aspects of the business to letting those things go and shifting into the management role, which is oversight, delegation, envisioning, communicating, and collaborating. It's a *lighter* feeling to the work versus the sensation of being up to your elbows in the mud of backend integrations, amateur graphic design, contracts and client onboarding, sales calls, the usual smorgasbord of life when you are the CEO, COO, CTO, CMO, sales team, and accountant for your business, but the work itself is still there.

One of the other things I want you to know is that when I went through this stage of having clients from hell and incredibly awkward and anxiety-producing situations, I grew exponentially.

Sometimes people think they need a new complex and automated business structure to hit seven figures, but what they really need is to sit in the fire of people's shit while running a people-centered business, to overcome all their fears of what they think will happen, and then realize that they can handle anything. The sense of empowerment that comes from going through the fire of the worst-case scenarios your mind creates and coming out stronger on the other side is what will make you a self-made man or woman.

> SOMETIMES PEOPLE THINK THEY NEED A NEW COMPLEX AND AUTOMATED BUSINESS STRUCTURE TO HIT SEVEN FIGURES, BUT WHAT THEY REALLY NEED IS TO SIT IN THE FIRE OF PEOPLE'S SHIT WHILE RUNNING A PEOPLE-CENTERED BUSINESS, TO OVERCOME ALL THEIR FEARS OF WHAT THEY THINK WILL HAPPEN, AND THEN REALIZE THAT THEY CAN HANDLE ANYTHING.

Truthfully, one of the things that terrified me about running a coaching business on a bigger level was knowing that people can be weird, and weird people-related situations give me a lot of anxiety. I am a recovering people pleaser and confrontation-averse type of soul, so I was always terrified of the possibility of someone not liking a program, asking for a refund, complaining about me behind my back to other clients, saying something mean about me on social media, or worse, pretending to love my work and then turning on me and saying how awful I was on the last day of our coaching and going on to shun and talk badly about me to everyone after that.

Unfortunately *and* fortunately, all of that has happened to me over the last several years and pretty much all of that has happened to my best clients, mentors, and friends who choose to play big in their businesses. Guess what? We all survive it and actually become better coaches and business leaders and way, way wealthier men and women on the other side of every single weird and uncomfortable situation.

Once I dealt with my literal worst nightmare of a client, I had my first six-figure month. Let me tell you why. I believe that in order to grow a business based on personal transformation like the one I run and you probably run or desire to run, you have to increase your capacity to hold people in the fire, through their ups and downs, and in a variety of emotional states, and you have to be a *safe place* for people to do this work if you want to be in this business long term. By navigating difficult conversations and difficult people and surviving it, you expand your capacity to hold the people you attract safely, and it therefore becomes more aligned for you to have more clients. And when it's aligned for you to have more clients and you're a genuine match for providing value and growth for them, they are given to you.

> **BY NAVIGATING DIFFICULT CONVERSATIONS AND DIFFICULT PEOPLE AND SURVIVING IT, YOU EXPAND YOUR CAPACITY TO HOLD THE PEOPLE YOU ATTRACT SAFELY, AND IT THEREFORE BECOMES MORE ALIGNED FOR YOU TO HAVE MORE CLIENTS.**

I don't believe any of this is required to have a high-level business, by the way. These days, I have zero client weirdness, zero refunds, zero anything at all except super soul-mate, high-achieving, results-getting, fun, and easy-to-serve clients who show up and do the work. It's the same with my team members. I officially have a no-drama-zone business. But it took going through some growing pains first: realizing places where I was out of alignment, where I could have shown up better, where I saw something early on and didn't speak into it, where I didn't set a boundary I needed to set, where I didn't let someone go who needed to be let go, where I saw a red flag in a sales call and took the client on anyway, and where I was scared to be imperfect as a leader and scared to mess up. Those situations taught me what I know to be true today: that I won't always get it right, but I can always do my best to make it right as soon as a mistake is made. That I can handle confrontation and someone not liking me or disagreeing with me. That I can be less than perfect and still be an amazing coach and deliver programs that help the vast, vast, vast majority of people get amazing outcomes. Those bumps in the road were the deepest healing parts of my journey and prepared me to be the leader I am today, to be able to hold the volume of clients I hold today, and to be able to hold them with a love and compassion that lets them feel safe to go through the very natural and normal ups and downs of transformation inside our container.

The last thing I'll share in this chapter is that right around the time I had my most difficult client scenario, a mentor taught me a concept from the counseling and therapeutic world that has stuck with me as a coach until present day: **the concept of unconditional positive regard for the client.** I noticed that when I chose to see my clients (and team members) in a positive, compassionate light, focusing on seeing them in their highest potential and emanating love toward them in all our interactions, even when they were having total meltdowns and projecting on me or completely forgetting to do something I asked them to do just a few hours previously, they actually showed up very differently. The drama dissolved. Between this and implementing clear, prerecorded onboarding modules for all my programs that set the container and set expectations between me and the client, taught them to get the most out of our work together, and taught them the principles my most successful clients have embodied that they, too, could use to get exceptional results, the stressful situations came to a halt.

And now I know that if any of those types of scenarios were to arise again, I know how to handle them, and there's something about just knowing you can handle the fire that keeps things cool, isn't there?

HOMEWORK FOR THIS CHAPTER

1. If you could have it any way you want it, who would be on your team and what support would you be receiving right now? What is one step you could take toward having more help right now?

2. Where do you need to better capacitate your existing team and put better onboarding and training materials for new hires into place so your people are set up to succeed and feel supported by you in their role? Your role is transitioning from supporting clients to supporting a team *and* your clients, so ask yourself on a daily basis, "How can I support my team to do their jobs and succeed today?"

3. Where are you over giving and overstepping your own boundaries with your clients or team members? Are you taking calls at crazy times? Providing access to you between sessions that isn't really a part of the agreement? Offering additional sessions? Discounting prices during your sales process? Doing trades or barters when you really just want to get paid cold hard cash for each sale you make? Clean it up.

4. You probably have a situation in your business right now (or have had one recently) where you just need to have an uncomfortable conversation, kick someone out of a program, say no, let someone go, refund someone who needs to be refunded, or set a new boundary . . . and you've been avoiding it. Create a plan to tackle this situation and lean into the discomfort of being the leader who does what's needed to be done to run your business in full alignment and integrity.

5. You really do get to have your business any way you want it. Create a new "rules of the kingdom" type of document where you declare exactly how things get to occur for you inside of your business. Examples include: My clients always pay on time. My clients are low maintenance and high achieving. My team is always one step ahead of the game. My offers always attract exactly the perfect number of people. My revenue is always increasing, month after month. Reiterate your declarations for your kingdom at least once a week by writing them out and reinforcing how your reality gets to be. It sounds crazy, but my mentors who have made over $20 million online have done this for years, and it's a big part of their success. When I started doing it too, you better believe those things started happening. (How I think it works is you simply train your brain to look for evidence of those things already occurring and train it to look for more ways to get those things to occur by coming up with new ideas or fresh angles on problem-solving that get you into alignment with that version of reality. I always have big, inspired ideas come through when I do my declarations in my journal.)

CHAPTER 13

GETTING IT "RIGHT": THE 1 PERCENT SHIFT FROM GREAT TO EXTRAORDINARY

UBUD, BALI, INDONESIA
JULY 5, 2021

There's a point in your business where you're trying to get it right, but that will only get you so far. The next big stage comes when you decide *you can't get it wrong.*

If you had told me two years ago that at some point I would be able to earn $100,000 in a single month, the idea would have been as laughable and earth shattering as you telling me Bali airport would shut down and that I wouldn't travel outside of Indonesia for two years due to a viral pandemic in 2020. Hilarious. Unthinkable. But it happened.

And not only that I would do it once, as if by some miraculous one-time feat of business intelligence, but over and over again continuously *every month*, I would have looked at you the way I might have looked at you drunk and wobbly in heels at some party in Cape Town or Barcelona in 2014 if you told me someday I'd never have another job or drink another glass of alcohol and eventually reside permanently in a spiritual community in Southeast Asia. Absurd!

If you had told me when I was twenty-nine that I would be a self-made millionaire at any point in my life, no less in two years, I'd have looked around at my moldy Bali bungalow with not even a single couch or single decorative object in the whole place, my declining net worth of all of $15,000, and my two suitcases of weathered belongings that I'd trekked around the world and back again with and asked you point blank, "Are you tripping?"

> THERE'S A POINT IN YOUR BUSINESS WHERE YOU'RE TRYING TO GET IT RIGHT, BUT THAT WILL ONLY GET YOU SO FAR. THE NEXT BIG STAGE COMES WHEN YOU DECIDE YOU CAN'T GET IT WRONG.

I grew up seeing my mom faithfully cut coupons on Sunday mornings with a big mug of Tim Hortons coffee planted next to the pile of newspapers as she flipped through them with furrowed brows. I think back to the $1,800 I saved, precious $25 paycheck by precious $25 paycheck from the age of fifteen to eighteen, sweeping floors and coming home stinking of chicken fingers for years on end. The years taking the subway home at 3 a.m. instead of taking a $15 cab ride in New York. The countless choices I made from scarcity, from the deeply entrenched insecurity that drove me to save pennies on the dollar for years because there was no safety net in my life.

I was my own plan B if the job didn't work out or if I got into trouble and my savings weren't enough. There was a toughness in me from that, an edge you couldn't quite catch in my free-spirited blog posts or under my business suits as I swiped my badge at IBM's offices on Wall Street.

There were rough patches on my heart from being born into a society where you're on your own and where you rely on money for survival, and if you weren't born into a rich family, that weight of survival rests very heavily on seventeen-year-old shoulders leaving the house for the first and last time like I did. Who put herself through university on a full scholarship and took the smart job afterward to get herself settled into a decent rung on the corporate ladder her parents could have never touched. Who then woke up, threw it all away for a faint soul-remembering, and proceeded to travel the world in search of the answers to bigger questions. Who staggered and stumbled on her path of entrepreneurship for four years before seeing any kind of monetary results.

What was required of me as a person and an emerging leader on the soul level to earn $100,000 in a single month is far more interesting for me to explain to you than how we earned it (and continuously, for years) as a business. I've always said that I didn't set out to make a million dollars. I was simply fascinated by the idea of *who* I would have to become in order to be a match for it.

And who did I have to become to play at these levels?

I had to soften the hard edges in my being.
I had to learn to accept support.
I had to give up my tendency and attachment to struggle.

For a while, I was the person who got it right. I studied the world of entrepreneurship with the same intensity I used to become fluent in Chinese, a tonal language where precision is essential to being understood.

> I'VE ALWAYS SAID THAT I DIDN'T SET OUT TO MAKE A MILLION DOLLARS. I WAS SIMPLY FASCINATED BY THE IDEA OF WHO I WOULD HAVE TO BECOME IN ORDER TO BE A MATCH FOR IT.

(By the end of my degree, I could read Chinese history in Chinese and write handwritten essays about the Cultural Revolution era, something to this day even millions of Chinese-born citizens can't do. The focus required for this level of mastery of something so foreign was extreme.) As a new entrepreneur, I sat on the sidelines and surveyed the landscape like a seasoned hunter studying the environment of its prey. I saw what my coach was doing, and I followed in her footsteps with the same degree of success. As I grew, I was quick to notice the trends in marketing and sales that seemed to create amazing results for others in my industry, and I replicated them expertly, with slight modifications to make these strategies feel like mine.

I honed my goals and income targets, and I achieved them quickly, as we've covered so far. But making what a well-trained corporate lawyer makes in a year in a single month is an economic feat, especially when most small businesses fail within the first year. Most women will never become millionaires. I had achieved what many aspire to but very few get to experience.

I don't say this to brag, I say it to pull back the curtain on *why* I was able to do it (and how you can too).

Because at some point well before I hit this milestone, I felt suffocated by my desire to get it right. To implement the online coaching model "correctly." To check all the boxes and do what was done by the other successful coaches.

The interesting thing was that I started noticing it in my clients first. I would become silently infuriated by how they would copy me or take my word so literally like it was verse from the Holy Bible or become agitated with me if I did something they didn't like or resonate with. It became mind-bogglingly annoying, and I sought counseling from my therapist to help me become less impacted by the actions and projections of my rapidly expanding client base that was starting to feel unbearably needy and codependent.

There were many times in this period when I wanted to give everyone their money back and close up shop, feeling that holding more people through transformation would become too energetically depleting. *Maybe I'm not built for this*, I admitted to myself and fought the temptation to chuck my phone into my new Olympic-sized swimming pool. As much as I wanted to grow to the next level, it wouldn't be worth it if I felt suffocated by my demanding clients who were constantly seeking my answers and approval for everything.

There were a few clients who I did fire during this period, thankfully. I happily released them back into the wild to find a new coach whom they could torment with their long, complaining emails and persistent sense of dissatisfaction with their lives that they projected onto me and my team. I started to politely and lovingly confront clients who were copying me and point it out to them without taking it personally, which actually invited our work to go deeper to ensure they were developing their own unique marketing instead of adopting mine and parroting a message and business style that wasn't truly their own.

I grew a bigger pair of balls, basically. I learned with my therapist to enforce boundaries like *no, I'm not answering your tenth question of the day* or *no, that's not included with the program*, and to enforce them without a charge of my past trauma behind it, like I was slamming my fist down or shaking a finger at my naughty child the way my mother did with me when I was young. (Tempting when you feel taken advantage of as a service provider, I know.) Instead, I learned to calmly iterate what the facts were and healthfully detach from any energetic backlash or temper tantrum they'd throw afterward.

Unsurprisingly, my client community upleveled, grew up, got the memo, and matched my energy as the coach who was growing past her judgments, reactivity, and countertransference. They even got better results when I stopped over giving, babying, and pleasing them. I also got really clear on my zone of genius being business strategy and not emotional counseling of any kind. I invited all my clients to work with a therapist or mindset coach separately so we could be very clear on what belonged inside our container and within my rightful zone of genius and what didn't. The gray area was often the cause of stress for me and dissatisfaction for the other person.

From what I know now, these are all the normal growing pains involved with rapid expansion of a human-centered business, especially one that holds people through transformation (to me, creating and scaling a business is the ultimate vehicle for personal growth). It was in this period that I did a lot of the inner work that allowed me to lighten the energetic load that each new person brought into my space so I could gradually and sometimes exponentially hold more people and share my expertise with them.

> YOUR GROWTH ISN'T LIKE SOLVING FOR THE LENGTH OF THE HYPOTENUSE IN A HIGH SCHOOL GEOMETRY EQUATION. IT'S WILD OUT HERE, AND YOU'VE GOT TO MAKE BUSINESS YOUR OWN IF YOU EXPECT TO BE A LEADER AND BE SUCCESSFUL.

If I stayed in my wagging finger energy and silently resented my clients, I wouldn't have been a match to lead more of them, as you might imagine.

What happened next was an illumination of a huge blind spot that was perhaps one of the causes of my miserable energetic meltdowns backstage in my coaching business, which was seeming to receive standing ovations from the outside world looking in. I saw that the clients who were irritating me the most were the ones who most wanted to *get it right*. They viewed me as having the answers and the formula for them to do the business correctly so as to get the incremental increases toward predictable success.

Where on earth had they gotten this crazy idea? This was entrepreneurship, folks. Your growth isn't like solving for the length of the hypotenuse in a high school geometry equation. It's wild out here, and you've got to make business your own if you expect to be a leader and be successful. Something was out of alignment.

Oh right, *me*.

I was still trying to get it right. I was looking at my coaches as if their recommendations were gospel. I was mimicking and parroting them in my own way. I was innovating only within a small acceptable bandwidth within the success formula I imagined existed. And I was growing tired and weary of that too. I was waking up again, hungry for a change, hungry for more of me to be at the controls as my rocket ship was taking off. I didn't want to turn heads because I was performing well and checking all the boxes I was supposed to check, I wanted to turn heads because people were seeing my soul.

I saw my terrible blind spot, I saw where this was running me into a wall, and I knew I had to shift.

I knew the color-between-the-lines vibe was only going to get me so far. I inherently came to understand that to be wildly successful in this personal brand business, I had to be a leader. The literal translation of that would be: one who does not follow. Me following industry blueprints and templates, filling in the blanks, and mimicking what caused success for others was literally the opposite of the energy of leadership. And leadership is the thing that brings in the money and the clients and the opportunities. It was also bringing in clients who behaved in a similar way, so if I wanted to uplevel my clientele and work with even more powerful (and high-paying) men and women, I would need to clean up my own act first.

The truth is, what causes wild levels of success for me and my mentors and anyone else you look up to—and what will unleash your wildest level of success—is looking inside and seeing what you want, how you want it to be, deciding that you get to have exactly that, and then creating it. The woman you look up to isn't successful because she has trendy gold foil graphics and sells digital courses for $2,222 each. She's successful because the gold feels true for her, her greatest joy is selling courses, and $2,222 is the price that feels good to her. You doing the same thing with the same price points with the same look won't make you successful. It'll actually delay your results.

I'm not successful because I charge a certain price or because I run masterminds or because I like to use professional brand photography and drone videos of my lifestyle in Bali on my Instagram. I do those things because they feel good to me. I'm successful because I listen to the unique things my heart desires, and I'm led from within. I start trends because I'm in tune with what I like and what's true for me, which is usually different from how it's broadly being done.

Despite the fact that I live on a hot tropical island where barefoot hippie style and cotton goddess dresses reign supreme, I like boots. And leather. And denim. And despite the fact that I drive a 109.5 cc Honda Scoopy, I sling a Louis Vuitton handbag over my wrist that costs twice what the scooter costs. I import bold jewelry that appeals to me from New York, and I rock it. Everything in my house matches my brand colors, and not because I matched my house to my website but because everything I choose is based on what I like, and I am the brand. It's all cohesive. I lead from within.

> THE TRUTH IS, WHAT CAUSES WILD LEVELS OF SUCCESS FOR ME AND MY MENTORS AND ANYONE ELSE YOU LOOK UP TO—AND WHAT WILL UNLEASH YOUR WILDEST LEVEL OF SUCCESS—IS LOOKING INSIDE AND SEEING WHAT YOU WANT, HOW YOU WANT IT TO BE, DECIDING THAT YOU GET TO HAVE EXACTLY THAT, AND THEN CREATING IT.

When I first launched my masterminds, I made them six months, which was the industry standard at the time. But six months felt too long for me once I started running programs, and three months felt too short, so I landed on five-month commitments. At the time, everyone arched their eyebrows at a five-month coaching container, but a little while later, five-month coaching programs were popping up everywhere.

Have you heard the story of the family who cuts their turkey in half for Thanksgiving, despite the American tradition to roast a turkey whole? One day, when the dutiful newlywed is preparing Thanksgiving, her husband asks her, "Honey, why did you cut the turkey in half?" and she replies, "That's how my mother always did it."

Curious, she gives her mother a ring and asks her, "Momma, Joe asked me why we always cut the turkey in half. Can you tell me why?"

Her mother replies, "Oh, honey, that's how your grandma always did it." Questioning the logic of her own response, the mother rings up the grandmother and asks, "Why do you cut the turkey in half at Thanksgiving?"

The grandmother responds, "Have you seen my oven? If I didn't cut it in half, the turkey would never fit!"

Sometimes we think replicating the formulas we see from our leaders will cause us to have the same levels of success as they've had, when they were only doing what worked best for them and being unapologetic about it.

That's what I had to learn at this stage of my growth, where I freed myself from the rules. I learned that my biggest results exist exclusively in the physical and energetic plane of the universe where I was true to my desires, where I decided I was no longer obligated to do certain things I thought I had to do to be successful, and where I decided exactly how it would be for me and chose to collapse time around having it.

For example, there came a point when I hit an absolute wall in signing off on social media content that my team was pulling from my repurposed bank of writing every month. I just couldn't do it anymore, and I longed for the day when the team would be able to know the exact right text and photos to select, and they would just nail it, and I wouldn't have to micromanage their use of commas or overzealous gold swirls in the Instagram graphics.

I had two options in that moment: I could decide that I still needed more time to streamline my backend systems and train the team and work toward having that seamless marketing sign-off be my reality, or I could simply say, "I'm done, today, and this gets to shift, *now*," and then let the pieces fall where they may and let everyone figure it out whose job it is to figure it out.

Guess which one I chose? The big-girl CEO move. I stopped micromanaging the sign-offs, full stop, and then let my team rise to the occasion.

It wasn't as easy as it sounds, by the way. I felt a lot like a recovering sugar addict being handcuffed and taken through a Parisian patisserie, tortured and drooling. What happened? Well, I chose to believe in them, I chose to commit to why I wanted it to be done this way instead, and everyone got it done. I got my seamless sign-offs. I improved a process by immediately upgrading it to the multimillion-dollar company way—way before we were one. Because when I looked into the future, I saw the final "someday" result I desired and decided that's how we were doing our marketing. The faster we can do it the "someday way," the faster we arrive and make that vision our reality today.

And while the version of me who didn't yet understand how to be a CEO and wanted to get her grubby little hands into every detail of the business was being healthfully restrained, another part of me was being remembered and let loose.

My crazy genius.

The part of me who was forgotten in the very serious authority-building, niche-establishing, business-scaling process that got me to the point where I could make six-figure months. It was only a bit later when I started to plateau at that income level (not a bad place to plateau, and I can't complain, but it was a plateau nonetheless) that I realized what had gotten me to this point was not going to take me any further.

I had to come home to my creative self. I had to get back to being primarily a writer, a thought leader, and a messenger. The business expansion would only follow the expansion of my self-expression, where I unleashed myself through the written and spoken word onto the internet, and naturally a portion of the people who were activated and inspired by the way I showed up would choose to buy my company's courses or hire me privately. *Of course.* Of course the more I expressed myself and shared my opinions and my values and my story, the more people would be magnetized to the light of my purest life-force energy.

Unlike what I had been doing before, I realized that I no longer needed to mathematically work out where the money was going to come from—through which exact offers and channels, or exactly how the most ideal clients were going to find me. I didn't need to do calculated lead generation or premeditated engagement strategies. All those things helped me to get here and can be helpful strategically at the early stages of establishing yourself as a business online, but I knew at that point, they wouldn't help me get *there*. They wouldn't help me manage a multimillion-dollar online education and coaching company that I ran virtually in my spare time and that nourished me as one of many vehicles of investment and contribution I had and made in the world. They wouldn't help me run a business that naturally continues to grow exponentially, multiply its revenue, and compound the individuals reached and served as a result.

To get there, I had to innovate, make up new strategies, create offers nobody's ever heard of before, use my team and collaborate in unconventional ways, and write more things that had nothing to do with the business but simply sought to put a spark of hope and possibility and magic into the hearts of my audience.

> YOUR FULLY UNLOCKED CREATIVE EXPRESSION IS WHAT LEADS TO GREATER WEALTH.

The paradox here is that those will be the very things that draw the most people into my business . . . and yours.

The creative genius gets to lead now. She gets to write books and stand on stage and cast off the chains and knock down the walls and make it however she wants it to be. She knows that's the most direct route to realizing the next level results and vision she sees inside.

Essentially, your fully unlocked creative expression is what leads to greater wealth.

Not more effort and more hours, not more ads, not all the new strategies, not being on all the platforms. The strategies and platforms are only in service to your voice, and that's the one true key to unlocking your next level.

The path from being a great entrepreneur to becoming *extraordinary* is a 1 percent shift. It's a tweak. I know this is how it was for me. That 1 percent tiny little millimeter of a shift came from taking everything that was already working in my business and simply deciding to be more of me behind it all. To radiate and permeate my essence through each crevice, each post, each decision. To more radically and powerfully back my desires. To more relentlessly say the thing that needs to be said. To be uncompromising in following my nudges and intuition. To change my mind when I need to change my mind and often shrug my shoulders and say, "This is just what's coming through, so this is what we're doing" to the team, and fully trusting it.

The biggest thing I help my clients do when they work with me is completely dismantle any ideas of how their business "should" look or how it's "supposed to be" structured in order to achieve a certain level of success or income. The reality is that in order to achieve unrealistic, impractical, wild, and extraordinary levels of success like you want to, you're going to have to completely build your business from the inside out: by listening to what you really want, how you want it to look, and who you want to work with, then deciding that you truly do get to have it that way. In fact, that's the way you *have to* have it if you're going to be successful.

Soul-mate clients want something fresh and something that feels very true to the person they are hiring because it gives *them* permission to have their business any way they want it, too. Look for mentors who won't tell you there's one path or one way to be successful and steer clear of the ones who want you to replicate their way of doing things. Hire the ones who support you with their expertise, knowledge of the market, and best practices that are like tools they bring out to support the vision and structures that make the most sense for you as an individual.

Likewise, look for clients who don't simply want a one-size-fits-all magic-pill formula from *you*, because they are set up for a long, hard ride from the beginning if they think that's what will make them successful—instead of trusting they will get to have the things they want no matter what and then focusing on enjoying the learning process and the journey to producing it.

Another 1 percent shift to look into when you feel like the next level you're destined for is right at your fingertips but just not dropping in or unfolding as rapidly as you'd like is your messaging. The thing is, you evolve quickly, so your business has to keep up. One tiny oversight might be that you're actually speaking to clients and sharing a message that's just a *slightly* outdated version of you and your work. And maybe you didn't even realize. The results you can get with an outdated message can be "fine," but if you want extraordinary results, you'll need to go in and do the internal check to see if there's a tweak, a pivot, or a truth that has updated inside of you that needs to now be revealed to the outside world and represented in your work. Continuously evolving your message in this way is the path to the next big results, visibility, financial success, opportunities, connections, support, and fulfillment you know are yours.

Lastly, one of my favorite tools for innovation is the practice of setting aside what I call "whitespace thinking time." I'll block off time on my calendar and bring a question to my brain like *I'm feeling a desire to talk about this topic of niching (for example) in a different way than what the dominant conversation in my wing of the industry has been so far. What is the new angle? What is the fresh concept or analogy or practice I want to bring through?* Then I sit and wait for the answer. I'll journal, I'll stare into space, I'll scribble on a whiteboard, I'll be with the not knowing, and I'll stay with it until something comes. Some of my best program names, offers, content pieces, and even this book came from whitespace thinking time.

HOMEWORK FOR THIS CHAPTER

1. Schedule time this week for whitespace thinking about an area you feel either inspired to talk about in a new way or a part of your business that's feeling dull and contrived and repetitive that you know needs tweaking (or a complete overhaul). Ask your brain to innovate on this area and bring a fresh perspective. It's amazing what new answers you'll get when you ask the right questions, even to your own brain.

2. Look at your business and ask yourself where you have been doing things in a way that you simply copied and pasted from a previous mentor or have kept doing something simply because you think you're "supposed to" do it in order to have things properly structured or because everyone else seems to have it. Where have you been sounding a little too much like someone else you look up to or have studied under? What might happen if you dismantled those pieces or at least stopped to question what they are doing inside your business if you're not feeling a full-body yes to them? What might want to come out if you stopped repeating parts of someone else's message? Here's your permission to break it apart and put it back together in a way that is much more fully aligned with who you know yourself to be and where you're going and how you want to get there (and how you want to feel as you go there).

3. Where are you trying to "get it right," maybe so much so that you're losing your voice, subduing your creative impulses, and dialing down the exact parts of you that are going to be what draws in your next huge wave of soul-mate clients? Come up with a plan to clean that up and start letting what needs to come through you just come through you and come out into the world.

4. What is, in fact, wanting to come through you right now? Is there a new product or offer idea that feels crazy but inspired and fully honest to who you are? Is there a piece of content that is ready to stream through your fingers onto the page, or something you feel compelled to get online and go live and share with your audience about? Practice tuning into this every single day, then doing it. Your million-dollar business model could be quite this simple.

5. If you knew all aspects of your business and the way you wanted things were just a done deal, what would you be doing then? Imagine that version of yourself, who already has the team, the six-figure months, the TEDx Talks, whatever it is you're calling in and excited about having next and see what the version of you who already has all those things is doing in your life and business. How is she (or he) being? How does she show up now in the world? What's her day-to-day like? Now, my challenge to you is: How can you do more of those things now? How can you be more

like this version of yourself today? Is there something she would create now that you aren't giving yourself permission to have or create until you've done all the other things first? For me, I knew the version of myself who is running a multimillion-dollar-per-year company would be writing a lot more from her heart. She'd be resting more. She'd be chilling and writing books and seeing only clients she really loved. She'd be so deep in trust of the next people coming in to buy whatever offers her team was selling for her that week. So, what prevents me from doing that now? Nothing. Is it actually the way to accelerate my path forward? Yes. Is that my primary multiple-seven-figure strategy now? Yes. Is it working? You betcha.

CHAPTER 14

BECOMING SELF-MADE FROM THE INSIDE OUT: A HEALTH REFORMATION

DOHA, QATAR
THE GRAND HYATT HOTEL
JUNE 13, 2015

I know precisely the last time I ever got drunk. And I know precisely how much this has contributed to my ability to generate the success my business has seen to this day.

In a country made almost entirely of oil and desert, boozy brunch in Doha was a *thing* as an expat. We didn't have a whole lot else to do.

After long work weeks consisting of mingling with the governor of the Central Bank of Qatar, meeting the CEOs of top Middle Eastern banks, and being invited to stay in six-star resorts owned by our clients, I looked forward to letting down my hair, putting on some high heels, and downing a few glasses of champagne.

I never had a drinking problem, if you consider binge drinking every weekend from the age of eighteen to twenty-five to be simply the normal course of maturation for American young adults. At university, we partied three to five nights a week (and I still graduated with two degrees in highest honors, fluent in multiple languages, and with a prestigious consulting job in New York City).

When I lived in China, I drank *baijiu* at karaoke clubs, played silly

Chinese dice games made exclusively for drunk people, and my Mandarin got more fluent the more inebriated I got. In Japan, I found the highest-end clubs and stayed out until 7 a.m. when the dutiful Japanese salarymen would be on the train headed to work while I wobbled home in my miniskirt, reeking of cigarette smoke. In Addis Ababa, I befriended the wildest circle of locals whose infamous "Tequila Tuesdays" would often result in needing to import more tequila to Ethiopia. I drank vodka in Mongolia in broad daylight. South Africa? I led the charge to the house-music clubs in Johannesburg's CBD, where even the most brazen foreigners wouldn't step foot in out of fear of being robbed or kidnapped on the way back to the suburbs. I once lost my passport as a twenty-one-year-old partying until dawn in Seoul and missed my flight home from South Korea.

Wherever I went, I tore it up. I was always relatively respectable, usually the friend still taking care of The Really Drunk Friend, but alcohol was the center of my social life for about seven years across sixty different countries. I loved the music, the adventure of socializing in new cultures, and the act itself of pretty much flinging myself nightly into a country's party scene and watching the shenanigans that would unfold. I lived for the Sunday morning stories. And I never second-guessed it. Partying like this appeared to be perfectly normal to me, and of course, I surrounded myself with other reckless young people who affirmed that norm.

This may seem like it's coming out of left field, but I couldn't tell you my story of becoming a self-made woman (and I couldn't prepare you for your own meteoric rise to success) without talking about the huge positive ripple effect that came after the moment I stopped drinking alcohol.

That last time happened when I was teetering around in heels at the Grand Hyatt Doha, drinking champagne at noon with the other members of Qatar's elite international expatriates and a few handsome members of the Welsh rugby team. The boys started fighting each other, I passed out in a cab on the way home, and a pervading sense of aloneness, dissonance, and dissatisfaction crept into my awareness when I woke up.

The next day, I quit.

I didn't expect to quit for good, mind you.

I just literally woke up. On so many levels.

I did something that Sunday morning that I had never felt drawn to do before: I researched the negative health effects of alcohol. I did a lot of reading, with my eyes opening a little wider with each link I opened. By the end of a few hours, I had decided I was going on a month-long break from drinking, which coincided with the holy month of Ramadan in Qatar (when there's no alcohol for sale in the entire country), and I also decided I needed to overhaul my diet.

Blueberries, I remember musing to myself. *I need to eat more blueberries.*

That month turned unexpectedly into exactly seven years from the publishing date of this book, which is how long it's been since I've had more than a glass of wine.

What happened back in Doha was an act of grace.

I started to feel the pull away from the vapid party scene and more toward this little blog I was working on growing. The hangovers had started to eat into my daylight on the weekends, which was the only time I had to focus on my side hustle and my ultimate long-term goal of being able to leave the advertising company I was working for and "do my own thing."

The sun rose on the awareness of the importance of my physical body and health in my life for the first time.

Two months later, I quit that company and traveled the world for a year and a half.

One of my first stops was India, where I had felt a spontaneous soul-stirring to do a ten-day silent Vipassana meditation (which was my first time meditating). I dove headfirst into the deep end, folks, and that led to an unexpected four-month immersion in India's finest spiritual sites and my first chapter as a vegetarian.

> MY DESIRE TO BECOME AN ENTREPRENEUR WAS, IN FACT, ACCELERATED BY MY DESIRE TO SPEND MONTHS OF UNINTERRUPTED TIME EVERY YEAR IN MY SPIRITUAL PRACTICE.

The teachers I met in Rishikesh in 2015 would become important figures in my life, and for the next four years, I would make an annual pilgrimage to India to study yoga and meditation. My desire to become an entrepreneur was, in fact, accelerated by my desire to spend months of uninterrupted time every year in my spiritual practice. I couldn't work or travel on anyone else's schedule anymore. The decision to create a business that would support this lifestyle—part monk and part online celebrity—was made.

The work I did around my health through yoga changed my life. I did ancient cleanses of my digestive system, which left me feeling more sensitive, intuitive, and clearer than I'd ever felt. I found myself happier, with fewer mood swings and more energy, on a light vegetarian diet.

After moving to Bali, the call to work on my health only deepened. I was soon coming home, padding around my parents' kitchen in Nepalese elephant pants and throwing things out of the food cupboard, much to their dismay. I replaced their canned items with fresh organic fruits and vegetables, cooked vegan meals for my steaks-on-the-grill-loving father, and brought them huge bottles of *ashwagandha* and *triphala* straight from the streets of New Delhi.

I continued to feel better, more myself. The appeal of alcohol, sugar, meat, and heavy foods was lost altogether and replaced by a vibrant effervescence, a fresh attunement to my body, and an emotional homecoming that was making my creativity blossom. It was in these days that I followed the intuition that led to healing my scoliosis and hiring my business coach. My skin radiated on my livestreams. My nervous system felt calm on sales calls. I had boundless energy to create content and channel brilliant ideas that made my income double. During this period, I entered a relationship after nine years being single, by no coincidence finding a man who was a vegetarian meditator and shared my same lineage of yoga.

This is where the journey of my health overlaps with our work together right here, friends.

I didn't touch a *drop* of alcohol for about four years after I spontaneously quit in Doha. I didn't eat meat for years, as well. To this day, I don't drink caffeinated coffee or eat sugar except on a special occasion. I've gone through periods of strict liver cleansing where I wouldn't eat dairy, gluten, or corn for months, followed by periods of relaxing the protocols and eating more intuitively. As much as I love pasta and parmesan (my real last name is Giolando, remember), I often made more money in the months without croissants and cheese, as if my magnetic field was purer and more amplified during my cleansing periods, if you believe in that sort of thing. I do.

And I also believe that the self-discipline I cultivated through my health practices, in addition to the enormous tangible benefits to my body, mind, and energetic field, have directly impacted me as an entrepreneur and as a woman.

AFTER YEARS OF FOLLOWING MY INTUITION, I DEEPLY TRUST MYSELF TO SAY NO AND STAY CONSISTENT WITH MY SACRED NOS IN ORDER TO SAY YES TO SOMETHING BIGGER: MORE ENERGY, MORE CREATIVITY, MORE CLARITY, BETTER HEALTH, AND A SHARPER MIND IN SERVICE OF MY HIGHER SELF AND HER GIFTS AND VISION.

Being able to quit alcohol overnight, *cold turkey*, after seven years of partying is extraordinary. I quit drinking regular coffee in much the same way after listening to the *Medical Medium* podcast episode on caffeine. Like literally stopped drinking a latte halfway through the episode and never picked it up again. (Is it any surprise I attract clients who invest six figures in working with me with the same level of clear, all-in, decided energy? Everything is connected.)

I don't know if I'll always be a no to sugar and cappuccinos, but right now, I am. After years of following my intuition, I deeply trust myself to say no and stay consistent with my sacred nos in order to say yes to something bigger: more energy, more creativity, more clarity, better health, and a sharper mind in service of my higher self and her gifts and vision.

Today I have a circle of friends in which almost no one drinks alcohol or coffee . . . imagine this in a world where it seems like everyone is on the roller coaster of uppers and downers. It's another reflection of my values manifesting into reality, and my alcohol-free friends are each the clearest beams of light you've ever seen (and grounded businessmen and women running successful companies of their own).

My regular health practice includes colon hydrotherapy once a month, daily celery juice, *Medical Medium* heavy metal detox smoothies (which have healed my heavy metals levels, and I have the laboratory tests to prove it), 85 percent vegetarian gluten-free sugar-free diet, and yearly liver and colon cleanses, supervised by my naturopath. Plus, weekly psychotherapy sessions, monthly energy healings and osteopathy sessions, semiweekly personal training sessions at the gym, and other general sensible self-care.

The truth is, as unrelated as it may seem, the healthier my physical body has become, the more money I've made. In periods when I'm eating even cleaner than I normally do, those are usually my biggest months. It seems to me that the purer my vessel is, the purer my message, my intuition, and my creative flow, and the more magnetic I am to the outside world. Besides the fact there is an uncanny correlation between my bottom-line results and the radiance of my physical body, my health is simply my number one priority. I can't run my company without the energy levels I have, the focus my brain is capable of, and the attunement to sensation within my body itself that provides the basis of my channeling and intuition that creates powerful conversations and results with my clients. When I hear a voice say, "Ask her about why she stopped painting" and I feel a prickle in my neck, I know that's what needs to be said to the client. It's my guidance system and my gift. Usually they will say, "I can't believe you'd mention that . . ." and reveal some long overdue spiritual guidance they've been receiving too.

I'm not saying you need to eat the same things I eat or follow any of the regimes or suggestions I've offered here. However, what is important is that you decide your values about food, alcohol, and health, determine what you're available and not available for, and continuously prioritize your mental clarity and physical well-being if you want to run a business sustainably over the long term at the levels we've been talking about in this book.

Self-care is a nonnegotiable that comes first, even before my creative output. It's a prerequisite. I fill up my own cup, then the overflow from me feeling good spills over into the business and leads to a positive feedback loop where I prioritize living my best life and caring for myself, which fills me up and then provides energy for the business. This is a system that keeps my cup permanently full instead of only doing self-care practices when I'm run down or need to compensate for a big push in the business. At Elaina Ray International, we don't do big pushes, we don't burn out, and we make self-care a priority for every client and team member.

Because we're in this for the long haul.

> YOU ATTRACT WHAT YOU ARE, NOT WHAT YOU WANT. AND IF YOU'RE BEING INCONSISTENT OR NONCOMMITTAL, REGARDLESS OF THE AREA OF LIFE IT'S RELATED TO, IT'LL CALL INCONSISTENT AND NONCOMMITTAL PEOPLE AND RESULTS INTO YOUR LIFE.

My philosophy around making health changes that may be helpful for you to keep in mind to stay motivated is to not focus on saying no to something I used to like, like fried chicken or gin and tonics, but to focus on saying yes to something else I want more, like a crystal-clear mind that channels brilliance for myself and other humans and boundless energy with zero crashes throughout the day. This mindset around change-making has always served me when I've become unavailable for certain things in my life that the majority of people elsewhere are rather unintentional about, and I feel like an alien for feeling called to choose something different. I simply stay focused on what I'm saying *yes* to instead.

> BUT I'M NOT DOING THINGS THE WAY THE VAST MAJORITY OF PEOPLE DO THEM. I GET RESULTS IN MY LIFE THAT ARE EXTRAORDINARY AND PUT ME ON A VERY ELITE PORTION OF THE BELL CURVE. I GET THE RESULTS MOST PEOPLE DON'T GET BECAUSE I'M WILLING TO DO THINGS MOST PEOPLE WON'T DO. IF YOU DEVELOP THE SAME ATTITUDE, YOU'LL SEE THE RESULTS.

One interesting thing I've noticed is how any energy of "wobble" in your life, even well outside of business, will affect the business. For example, have you ever had clients come in only to then start feeling unsure about whether your program is really a fit for them? Or have you had people on sales calls who always need to "think about it," only to never come back again? Or maybe you've had people tell you they are in, only to then disappear without putting down the deposit. Sound familiar? I thought so, because I've been there, and when I shifted how I showed up, for myself first and foremost, everything else aligned as a result. Situations like these where the other person is exhibiting flakiness, inconsistency, or wobbliness are likely a reflection of you holding wobbliness inside of you. Perhaps you said you were going to go vegetarian for three months but then you snuck in a hot dog, or you decided to give up alcohol for a month but caved for a glass of Pinot Noir after two weeks. Those actions unfortunately affect your magnetism because you attract what you are, not what you want. And if you're being inconsistent or noncommittal, regardless of the area of life it's related to, it'll call inconsistent and noncommittal people and results into your life. Because you're a match for that. This is the reason I'm able to attract very committed clients who show up ready to invest, pay in full, and excel throughout the container. I'm a match for that. I hold that vibe in all areas of my life.

Note: I understand that my approach to health may also be more strict or intense than what makes sense or sounds appealing to the vast majority of people, perhaps including you. I understand that the vast majority of humans drink alcohol and coffee and eat meat indiscriminately and seem to be doing just fine. But I'm not doing things the way the vast majority of people do them. I get results in my life that are extraordinary and put me on a very elite portion of the bell curve. I get the results most people don't get because I'm willing to do things most people won't do. If you develop the same attitude, you'll see the results.

Almost everyone out there wants more clients and more money and more freedom and more time and more opportunities; they have big dreams and talk a big talk. Very few people will actually achieve those things, not because they aren't capable or it's not in the cards for them, but simply because they don't do the things it really takes to get there, consistently. They don't take the risks, make the hard decisions, follow their intuition, do the healing work, think consciously about their relationship to things like food and money and their bodies, and they don't show up every day even when it looks like the thing they want will never happen.

The people like you and me who achieve those things? We show up, we walk through the voids, we take the risks, we leave our safe jobs, we take out loans and get second jobs to back ourselves, we put ourselves out there vulnerably, we say things we're scared to say, we create relentlessly, we hire support before we're ready, we make bold moves, we ask for things most people wouldn't ask for, and we do it day in and day out no matter what until the vision comes to life.

HOMEWORK FOR THIS CHAPTER

1. What is your current daily and weekly self-care regime? Where does it need some improvement? Add one thing at a time, integrate that over a seven-day period, then add one more thing. Deciding to make five changes at once will likely cause you to break trust with yourself when you understandably cannot keep up with all those modifications simultaneously. It's better to decide to do one thing consistently than to break trust with yourself.

2. Where are you being wobbly with your own intentions around your health and well-being? Clean it up.

3. Practice using your intuition right now. What is one thing you're consuming right now that is inhibiting your exponential growth? What is in the way of you becoming who you know you're meant to become? How do you need to modify or eliminate your relationship to this thing in order to improve your life and the results you're getting?

CHAPTER 15

UNDERSTANDING THE PARADOX OF GROWTH

UBUD, BALI, INDONESIA
NOVEMBER 15, 2021

I was recently speaking to a good friend and fellow entrepreneur who was making one of the gravest and most easily made mistakes in the game: He was in a rush.

He's in a good industry but has woven together the story that *it's now or never. We have to move fast to make our fortune now.* It felt like he was bracing himself against the future, creating the money that he felt would finally provide security for him and his family.

In response to such a dire, fast-paced, do-or-die story, he was working a lot. Twelve-hour days, seven days a week. His partner was concerned, and the two of them wound up at lunch with me one sunny afternoon in Balinese paradise, where I fortunately got to talk some sense into him.

Here's what I shared.

After years of helping hundreds of men and women grow their own businesses and create financial freedom, I've seen two main archetypes of clients:

Type One comes in with finger-snapping energy, wanting her results and wanting them fast, virtually demanding a quantum leap from the universe and putting herself on a timeline to get it done by a certain date with a certain number of dollars or else it's going to mean something about her and her future. She's very focused on the monthly income goals, the numerical outcome of launches, and *speed*. She wonders, in the back of her mind, if it will really work out for her at all.

Type Two comes in with the same ambition in a different flavor. She also wants to create big business results, have clear financial outcomes, and move as quickly as possible. However, she sees the bigger picture. She knows she's in this for the long haul. She sets herself up to make a substantial investment in herself and the business with some energetic and financial cushion around it so it never feels adrenaline-fueled with a false sense of make-or-break. She doesn't need the results to come on a specific timeline, and she's willing to do whatever it takes, for as long as it takes, until it works. She knows it's not *if* but *when* it will work, so she focuses on enjoying the process: learning new skills, understanding her market, experimenting with our new strategies in a playful, curious way, and prioritizing her growth as the person behind the business above all else.

Who do you think gets the fastest, biggest, wildest results?

My Type Two client is exercising what I've come to term the *paradox of patience*. Ironically, because she's willing to stay the course and play for as long as it takes and she's enjoying the ride, the relaxedness of her state of being becomes a match for receiving. The universe has fewer lessons that this woman needs to learn before she can receive her abundance and move on to the next level of growth and learning. She is slowed down and grateful, present, lighthearted, and committed to the process instead of being attached to a specific outcome. She is oriented around the big picture, willing and able to follow through, and open to learn and receive support, all qualities we need more of in the world.

> HER SECURITY COMES FROM KNOWING WHO SHE IS.

The Type One client has many lessons to learn and providing her with money, success, and affirmation would have only corroborated with unhelpful and antiquated ways of being that we need to outgrow as a human race: a lack of presence and absence of gratitude while racing to the next achievement out of a lack of true self-worth, relying on money to provide a feeling of security, taking things too seriously, rushing through our precious lives, and the list goes on. By withholding money and the business results she so desperately wants (which would only serve to temporarily fill a hole in her being), the universe gets her attention and can facilitate a healing of the soul-level voids and core wounds that will elevate her consciousness and upgrade her character and core identity in a way that will ripple positively through many lifetimes. This is the more important work than the mere business growth.

Sometimes it's a hard, long, windy, uncomfortable road for this type of person if they are more resistant to the soul-level work required to be successful in an aligned and sustainable way in this life. Ultimately, and especially if she's a client receiving my careful mentorship and expert eyes that see bigger patterns like these, she'll wake up, receive the message, make the shifts, and then her results will come.

> SUCCESS AND WEALTH RESPOND TO WHO WE ARE, NOT JUST WHAT WE DO.

The Type Two client doesn't have the false sense of money providing security, so she moves faster without unnecessary roadblocks. Her security comes from knowing who she is. She understands and respects her character: her discipline, her willingness to really go for it, her magic and gifts, her ability to communicate and advocate for herself and her desires, her clear and sharp intuition, and her confidence in building relationships. These are the qualities that will continue to attract money in a fluid way throughout her lifetime—regardless of the state of the economy, one particular business venture or, in fact, anything outside of herself and outside of her control.

Her character is within her control. Her core identity is what she cultivates with the love and attentive focus of a mother smiling and radiating that love down onto her newborn, like how our great-grandmothers tended to their gardens. We are in charge. Money will flow to us and through us abundantly by way of responding to our core identity as entrepreneurs.

This must be the focus of the work. Success and wealth respond to who we are, not just what we do.

I know if this business doesn't work out, I'll create the next one. I've already failed so many times on my way here, so I can fail again, be okay, then move on to the next thing. I know myself to be a risk-taker, a bold-mover, and a highly intuitive and perceptive woman. I know my level of integrity and the love I bring to my clients, team, and community. I feel my commitment to my mission in my bones. I show up every single day and I do what I say I'm going to do. I come up with brilliant ideas, *and* I execute on them. I don't hide behind perfectionism; I get things that matter to me done. I communicate with sensitivity and sharpness and channel the most incredible insights through my writings and live teachings. I prioritize my health, feminine radiance, and spiritual-healing work.

THESE ARE THE ASPECTS OF MYSELF THAT I KNOW HAVE ATTRACTED THE WEALTH I'VE CREATED. IF TODAY'S WEALTH WERE TO SOMEHOW DISAPPEAR, THESE ARE THE QUALITIES THAT WOULD MAKE IT BACK, TENFOLD.

WHO I KNOW MYSELF TO BE IS WHAT'S MADE ME A SELF-MADE WOMAN.

AND NOTHING CAN FUCK WITH THAT.

These are the qualities I hold dear about myself, and I continue to cultivate them. These are the aspects of myself that I know have attracted the wealth I've created. If today's wealth were to somehow disappear, these are the qualities that would make it back, tenfold.

Who I know myself to be is what's made me a self-made woman.

And nothing can fuck with that.

> I FIND THE EMOTIONAL STATES OF WONDER, SATIATION, SUFFICIENCY, PEACE, AND GRATITUDE TO BE THE EMOTIONS MOST COMPATIBLE WITH WEALTH AND FINANCIAL GROWTH SPURTS. THIS IS THE PARADOX OF GROWTH AS I CALL IT: THE MORE YOU CAN CONSISTENTLY RESIDE IN AN ENERGY OF PEACE AND SATISFACTION WITH WHAT YOU HAVE, THE MORE YOU WILL ATTRACT AND CREATE.

I myself have had periods of time playing in both camps of the two archetypes.

Yet the periods of time when I've experienced the greatest growth spurts in financial abundance came when I was most satisfied, grateful, and present with where I was in that moment.

The mornings when I would wake up and lie leisurely in the sun, listening to the sounds of Bali waking up with insects rattling, birds singing, frogs croaking, dogs barking, babies crying in the distance would be my most lucrative days. I would feel such enormous surges of joy as I looked around at the home I own in a tropical paradise, with the beautiful, handpicked colored pillows sitting on my couch and my furry, whiskered beasts prowling around our garden chasing dragonflies, happy as animals can be, and I would think to myself: *I've made it.* The nights where I'd float in my pool, staring up at the stars in wonder were the same nights I'd check my email and see large pay-in-full payments come in or a surprise soul-mate client sending in an application for private coaching.

I find the emotional states of wonder, satiation, sufficiency, peace, and gratitude to be the emotions most compatible with wealth and financial growth spurts. This is the *paradox of growth* as I call it: The more you can consistently reside in an energy of peace and satisfaction with what you have, the more you will attract and create.

Essentially, you have to feel like you've made it in order to make it.

I never created more money or attracted more clients or grew the business by feeling like what I had was insufficient or taking it for granted. The bratty periods where I felt $100,000 months weren't enough because the mentors I looked up to were making $300,000 were precisely the months when I would stall, feel like I was plateauing, or worse, sliding backward. The universe was not going to reward that mindset and was letting me know that I was beginning to play the game on a slippery slope, where a number was just a number and it always had to grow bigger or else it would be perceived as lack. I was trying to feed my ego and fill a void in those states. The greater order was not having any of it. I was perfectly allowed to make $300,000 per month; the money wasn't the issue, it was the energy behind it. I was allowed more, undoubtedly, but the story behind wanting more had to be aligned.

I learned to watch my stories very carefully.

> IF I FELT FULL, THE ENERGETIC EXPERIENCE OF FULLNESS SEEMED TO ATTRACT MORE.

I learned to play the game on grounded soil, where I could receive more while taking care that there was no void that the money and success would simply fall into and disappear. To close the void is very simple, I learned. I simply had to hold what I already had. My hands and heart had to be full of goodness and awareness of what I was holding, and my mind had to decide that it was plenty. If I felt full, the energetic experience of fullness seemed to attract more. And fullness on top of something that's already full creates *overflow*. Abundance. More than enough.

> OUR FINANCIAL GROWTH CAN BE A SPIRITUAL JOURNEY EVERY STEP OF THE WAY IF WE CHOOSE IT TO BE, ALLOWING OUR SOUL-LEVEL HEALING TO, IN FACT, BE FACILITATED BY OUR ASPIRATIONS TO BE WEALTHY, RESOURCED, RECOGNIZED, AND SUCCESSFUL IN OUR CHOSEN MISSION. CONTRARY TO SOME POPULAR BELIEFS I REFUSE TO ADOPT, THE DESIRE FOR WEALTH AND SUCCESS IS NOT AN OBSTACLE TO SPIRITUAL GROWTH BUT A TOOL TO SUPPORT OUR CONTINUOUS EVOLUTION AS A HUMAN BEING, CREATIVE GENIUS, AND LEADER.

If I felt "I have more than enough," then I received more. If I felt "This isn't good enough, I need more," I would receive less.

I had to simultaneously hold my desire for more expansion with the paradoxical feeling of being completely whole, fine, attended to, provided for, and held as I was, without any change at all. *That's* what created change and upward momentum. How funny! I love paradoxes.

Our financial growth can be a spiritual journey every step of the way if we choose it to be, allowing our soul-level healing to, in fact, be facilitated by our aspirations to be wealthy, resourced, recognized, and successful in our chosen mission. Contrary to some popular beliefs I refuse to adopt, the desire for wealth and success is not an obstacle to spiritual growth but a tool to support our continuous evolution as a human being, creative genius, and leader.

HOMEWORK FOR THIS CHAPTER

1. Where can you step into the energy of "I am good enough, I am doing enough, I have enough" more in your life right now, while still simultaneously holding the desire for expansion and knowing that you'll continue to get better, evolve as a person and business owner, have more abundance, and do more cool things? How would you show up today if you showed up from the energy of *sufficiency* instead of scrambling to get the next thing done because you feel not good enough if you don't have it already?

2. One of my favorite ways to increase money flow is by practicing gratitude for every single dollar that comes into my business. If I make a $22 sale off a tripwire, I'll take the moment to stop when I see the Stripe notification and feel grateful for it, as well as to acknowledge the person behind the purchase who is choosing to take a step forward today. If I receive a $22,000 pay-in-full, I'll do the same. My focus is on connecting to the souls who are taking action and who I am serving, directly or indirectly, through each dollar that comes in, rather than the dollars themselves. This practice of gratitude and acknowledgment has resulted in huge waves of growth, but more importantly, it has allowed me to feel more connected to my work and the lives I'm touching. I'm

more present with what I'm doing than just steamrolling through the next launch and taking the income and interest in my work for granted. Practice this for the next thirty days and document the impact on your income.

3. How might you be attached to certain outcomes and timelines for achieving your goals right now? How could you shift into more commitment to yourself, your journey, your learning, and your pure creativity in a way that feels more process oriented than outcome oriented? How might you feel differently behind the scenes of your business if you were to embrace that more?

4. Are you in a rush in any area of your business or your life? Are you fixated on a timeline somewhere, perhaps around the idea of how old you want to be when you get married or have kids, or around the age you want to be when you publish your first book, own your own home, or make your first million? Is the timeline and story around being too young, too old, or already "behind" serving you in achieving this goal? How might things shift if you decided to trust that the thing you desire is coming, and it's coming in its divinely arranged timing, and now you get to relax into living your best life while it emerges? A little more faith and a little more presence with *what is* can go a long way.

CHAPTER 16

HEARTBREAK, LOSS, AND COMING UNDONE

IBIZA, SPAIN
JANUARY 8, 2022

This wasn't meant to be one of the chapters in this book, but as they say, who you are when you start writing a book isn't who you are when you finish.

At this very moment of writing, I'm in the midst of a painful separation from my beloved, René, a statement I never thought I'd make. I've seen our wedding day countless times in my head, heard him say "I want to love you until you're old" so often, and built a literal home and a carefully constructed shared life with him over the last two and a half years. He even bought a ring.

Right now, I'm practicing what my therapist invited me to do: to come undone. To not know, to not feel like everything is going to be okay, to not be sure, to not see the next step, to not feel in control and in charge like I'm used to in every other area of my life. To surrender to the pain, to the disintegration of a love and a primary relationship that has held me sweetly for the last several years.

Only by coming undone at times can we later reassemble ourselves in a more aligned and integrated fashion. Sometimes it's by completely falling apart that we expand the way and to the degree we're meant to—and even required—for our next iteration. Sometimes the floor needs to fully fall out from under us in order to land where we're meant to land.

This is one of those times for me.

So, what happened you ask?

A gradual, unfortunate, inevitable breakdown of our shared vision for the future.

Here's the post I shared on Facebook the day after our uncoupling ceremony:

 Elaina Ray is at **Love.**
5 January

René and I are uncoupling.

It's with a heavy heart still full of a lot of love and a tear-streaked face that I write this post.

We've come to the end of the road in the romantic partnership portion of our best friendship.

René is certainly one of my soul mates in this life, and I couldn't be more grateful for the profound healing and transformational quality of our relationship.

It's been uplifting, positive, profound, and the best thing that's ever happened to me.

It just wasn't meant for forever, as much as we both wanted it to be and lived in the fantasy of what we thought we were or could be. I've envisioned our wedding day countless times in my mind, so clearly that it felt inevitable, and it pains me greatly to know that that's not our destiny.

The truth is, our shared vision of our future broke down a while ago, and we've been furiously trying to save "us," our magical third entity, behind the scenes. We've been to therapy, we've done the inner work, we've communicated like champions, we've gotten support from friends. We've given it our all.

The simple fact is that sometimes love just isn't enough.

René wants a baby in the near future, badly, and I don't.

Irreconcilable differences and, woefully, nonaligned life paths for marriage.

It's a truth neither of us have 100 percent certainty around, naturally, as many things in the next few years could change, but at the same time, it's something we sense in our bones.

He and I both have enough experience trusting whispers of irresponsible, reckless, wild, wonderful, intuitive knowing that it's something at this point we simply must listen to and trust that we're being guided in the direction of what's in the highest good for each of our soul's paths and the highest good of all beings.

I've been praying a lot over this decision to set my man free to **become a father and to set myself free to find one of my other** soul mates who will align with the woman I have become today, a woman I was not when I entered into this partnership two and a half years ago. I'm trusting I will be met in my newly emerging desires, and that everything I am seeking is seeking me back.

And it means walking into the abyss.

Letting go of this man's hand, which has held mine thousands of times inside the warm cocoon of a love that is so special indeed and walking into an uncomfortable unknown chapter of my life.

It means risking everything for a truth I can only feel in the subtle stillness where my soul feels most free and where I feel most true to myself.

It means saying goodbye in a way I've said goodbye to places, jobs, businesses, and other parts of my life that have, without fail, led me to the best success and greatest treasures of my life that I couldn't see coming.

I know I must say goodbye now and trust in that process unfolding **in my love life as well,** as difficult as that is to see or believe in this moment.

René:

Thank you dearly for these two and a half years. I love you so much and always will. Now we get to be best friends instead of lovers and partners. I have the utmost faith that we can uncouple gracefully and stay in each other's lives in the right order of things.

Thank you for showing me the beauty of a man who goes so all in on his woman, who's so committed and so loving. You've proved to many women (and men) around us that it's possible.

> Your love proves to me that because I attracted this frequency of sacred union once, I'll attract it again, and so will you.
>
> Thank you for traveling the world with me: Sweden, Thailand, Vietnam, Bali, Dubai, the Netherlands, Spain . . . we've had an international romance I treasure.
>
> Thank you for holding me countless times as I cried and purged my grief from the past. Being seen and supported in my pain in that intimate way has changed my life.
>
> Thank you for not giving a flying fuck how much money I make because when you met me, I was broke, and you watched my business explode and me transform into a financially evolved adult businesswoman, and you loved me all the same, every step of the way.
>
> Thank you for surviving a pandemic with me in a foreign country and being the best teammate through the weirdest and most stressful time the world has ever seen.
>
> Thank you for helping me build my dream home and first real estate investment in Bali. I would never have had the guts to go all in and buy a property (and another one) and build a goddamn extension on it without your encouragement and expertise.
>
> Thank you for your kindness, gentleness, positivity, and generosity with me and those around us. It's admirable, and your relaxed good-naturedness is something that's rubbed off on me and will be a primary quality I seek in my next relationship.
>
> And so much more I couldn't possibly continue to elaborate on here. You're a rock-solid man with a heart of gold, and you've been a magical blessing in my life.
>
> Here's to the next chapter for both of us.
>
> In my truth and yours, I trust.
>
> Love,
>
> Elaina

At first, we were on the same page: both a no to having kids. Then, about a year ago, René voiced out that he thought he might really want to be a father, which threw me into a portal of pain, denial, and confusion around my own desires. Every time it came up, I would have to cry my eyes out, isolate myself, and really ask my soul what I want. In the stillness of my own space and energy, the answer always came up: right now, I'm a no to being a mother.

Then I'd have to muster up all the courage I have, as someone who wants more than anything to be partnered for life with her one true love, and at the risk of losing everything, I would tell him with a strength I didn't know I had: "Babe, I love you so much. And I don't want kids anytime soon, so if that's something you absolutely must go and do, then I bless you and set you free." And each time he would come back and say, "I choose you. I want to do this with you. I'm okay either way."

Until he wasn't.

So, we went to therapy for six more months, asked the hard questions, searched for the clearest truth each of us could find on our own, and then made the ultimate decision that we were no longer aligned romantic partners. I spent my 2021 New Year's Eve wandering around Barcelona with René, weeping behind my huge Louis Vuitton sunglasses, realizing that the relationship I had placed all the faith in the world in was dissolving before my eyes. Or it already had.

Here's the thing and why I'm pouring out my heart to you about this: it relates to everything about being self-made and being a woman who knows her truth, listens to her truth, and moves based on that.

Do I know with absolute certainty that I don't want kids? No, but at this moment, that's the best sense I have. Does René know with absolute certainty that he must have children in order to fulfill his life's purpose? No, he doesn't know either, but at this moment, that's the best sense he has in his heart.

We could both be making huge, irresponsible, life-altering decisions we'll regret forever.

But I think somewhere deep down, we are choosing to have faith and to leap into the unknown on the basis of no more than a subtle prickle of the hairs on our arms when we think about life a certain way.

YOU PROBABLY HAVE SOME SIMILAR WHISPER IN YOUR LIFE AT THIS MOMENT THAT SAYS, "YES, THIS IS GOOD, BUT IT'S NOT QUITE IT." AND IT'S YOUR JOB TO CHOOSE TO EITHER BELIEVE THAT WHISPER AND FOLLOW WHERE IT LEADS YOU, WITHOUT QUESTION AND WITHOUT ANY CERTAINTY OR GUARANTEE, OR DO YOUR BEST TO IGNORE IT AND SEE HOW LONG YOU CAN HANG ONTO YOUR HEALTH AND HAPPINESS BY A SLIPPERY THREAD. YOU CAN EITHER FEEL CONFUSED AND WONDER, QUESTION, AND SECOND-GUESS YOURSELF, OR YOU CAN CHOOSE TO TRUST YOURSELF, DEEPLY. UNCONDITIONALLY.

We both know the thing we really desire, like really, really desire, is out there. But we have to say goodbye to each other, to something that's really good, really beautiful, really amazing, and just about perfect to be available for it.

Because it's not perfect. There's a huge, unmet desire in this relationship that's been swept under the carpet in the name of allowing ourselves to live in the fantasy of what we imagined we were or could be. There is, and perhaps always has been, some tingling, itching sensation in my body that says, "This is a good relationship, Elaina, but it's just not quite *it*."

That's the uncomfortable truth of being the kind of woman I am and the kind of person you probably are too.

You probably have some similar whisper in your life at this moment that says, "Yes, this is good, but it's not quite *it*." And it's your job to choose to either believe that whisper and follow where it leads you, without question and without any certainty or guarantee, or do your best to ignore it and see how long you can hang onto your health and happiness by a slippery thread. You can either feel confused and wonder, question, and second-guess yourself, or you can choose to trust yourself, deeply. Unconditionally.

In my experience, listening to the whisper, the blind faith you feel in your bones around something, whether it's regarding your job or your partner or where you live or something you want to see or do or make before you die, leads to the path of your highest good and the highest order of all beings.

This is the prayer I make in times like these, and one I'm making daily right now as I regularly sit across the table from René, in Spain, as we delicately uncouple ourselves and sob publicly in a variety of tapas restaurants and terrace cervecerias:

God, angels, universe, please help me to get clarity around this to the best of my ability. I'm just a human who is utterly blind seeing into the future, and I'm absolutely terrified of getting it wrong. You are all-knowing, and you know what's in the greatest good for me and all beings. Please guide me in the direction of what's best for me. Please be ever so gentle with me. I'm willing to see and do what needs to be seen and done, but I need a sign. I need a nudge. I need a little direction. I am open and ready. Show me the next step, and I will trust, and I will take it. Help me bolster my faith in this moment of need and help me see that everything is and will be unfolding for my greater good.

Should this prayer inspire or serve you, feel free to borrow it. Whether you believe you're talking to God or your higher self or accessing your subconscious or whatever feels true and comforting for you, it doesn't matter, just allow it to feel good and supportive to you.

Whether you need the help to leave a job, start a business, make a big investment in your business, shift careers, start a family, leave a marriage, move overseas, or any other major (or minor) life decision, let this prayer and your adaptation of it in any way that serves you be the invisible hand that can come and hold yours in times of pain, confusion, and need.

YOU ARE SO LOVED. YOU ARE SO SUPPORTED. YOU ARE NOT ALONE. THERE IS A GREATER ORDER TO WHAT'S OCCURRING THROUGH YOU AND AROUND YOU AND ALWAYS FOR YOU. EVERYTHING YOU WANT, WANTS YOU. YOU'RE WORTHY OF THE DESIRES THAT COME TO YOU IN WILD WHISPERS, AND IT'S SAFE TO LISTEN TO THE GUIDANCE THAT COMES FROM SOMEWHERE THAT FEELS IRRESPONSIBLE, IMPULSIVE, AND DEEPLY RIGHT.

From all the flying leaps I've taken, to leave my previous safe, good, almost perfect corporate jobs, to get fired and choose to start a business, to move across the world to start a new life, to travel the world alone many times over, this is by far the hardest. My heartbreak feels bottomless, and yet I know in my bones that I will be okay. I'll be more than okay. I'm going to be thriving on the other side of this rupture.

From the wellspring of my deep sadness, my bleary eyes, my tear-streaked face, and my shaky hands that write this for you and me both, here's what I know to be true:

You are so loved. You are so supported. You are not alone. There is a greater order to what's occurring through you and around you and always *for you*. Everything you want, wants you. You're worthy of the desires that come to you in wild whispers, and it's safe to listen to the guidance that comes from somewhere that feels irresponsible, impulsive, and deeply *right*.

Here's the other thing: One of the reasons that stalls us humans in making big, important realigning decisions in our lives is the fear of getting it wrong.

The decision to end this relationship is one René and I have both stalled on for as long as possible because of the deep, impractical love that connects us and the big desire for lifelong soul-mate love—as well as the big fear of getting it wrong.

How do we know for sure what our feelings are about children and the future three to seven years from now when life right now feels wonderful and complete?

We don't, really. All we know is the truth of this moment: For him to continue to be satisfied in a committed relationship, he needs to know that he's with a woman who wants to have children with him in the next three years or so. My truth of the moment is that *right now*, I can't promise that or stay in a relationship where I feel a pressure to commit to something that's never been an innate desire or aspiration of mine. What I really desire is a sacred union relationship and eventual marriage with a lifelong soul-mate partner who would be happy with kids or without them.

Of course, I'm still open to a change of heart later down the road, as many unlikely things have occurred and pleasantly surprised me in my life. Perhaps kids will be one of them—or not. But I'm not expecting myself to change my mind anymore. I'm not making myself feel wrong because my sense is different from other women's senses around this topic. The world often thinks women who don't want kids should or will change their minds. Don't expect me to, and I don't want to be with a partner who is expecting me to either. I sense that when I'm set free of expectation around this, my ultimate truth will safely emerge.

The most important underlying matter of this chapter, and this book as a whole, is the theme of self-trust. I deeply trust myself.

Here's the thing: I don't always feel actual *feelings* of trust in myself, but I choose to act in a way that I would act if I did trust myself. That's how I built the muscle of trust inside my relationship. When I first met René, I didn't actually feel trust in him, I just had to trust him if we were going to be in a relationship. It was another blind leap. Over time, my choosing to act as though I trusted him created situations where he proved very trustworthy to me, and over time, I felt the actual sensation and emotional quality of trust emerge between us.

Our relationship to ourselves is quite similar. At the beginning of the journey, you won't inherently feel completely trusting of yourself and your whispers. You'll feel confused and doubtful and wonder if you're hearing yourself right. As someone who's done a lot of therapy, trauma work, energy healing, and healing modalities of all kinds, here's what I've found to be true: There's a part of you that always knows. There's a part of you that has been greatly supported and directed despite the circumstances of your past. You are not broken, and you know your truth.

You can always choose to act as if you trust yourself (ask: What would I do if I couldn't get it wrong? What would I do if I deeply trusted myself?), and leap. And then watch as the evidence from life emerges to show you that you are trustworthy. You flex the muscle, and it grows stronger. It gets a bit easier every time and you get more familiar with the fear and discomfort, but the fear and discomfort never completely go away.

I'll repeat what I wrote above: You are so loved. You are so supported. You are not alone. There is a greater order to what's occurring through you and around you and always *for you*. Everything you want, wants you. You're worthy of the desires that come to you in wild whispers, and it's safe to listen to the guidance that comes from somewhere that feels irresponsible, impulsive, and deeply *right*.

These are the self-trusting moves you will have to make in order to become self-made in an aligned way that serves your greatest good and the greatest good of those around you.

And sometimes you're still not sure and strong enough, so you borrow evidence from those around you, like me. You listen to the sound of our voices and our souls before we go to leap, and you recognize the sound of trepidation, fear, and heartbreak . . . and you relate. Then you listen to the sound of our voices and souls after we leap, and you recognize the sound of aliveness, power, surrender, and rightness. You receive the transmission of *all is well on the other side*, and so you leap too.

Here's the post I wrote two months after my breakup (two months after writing this original chapter) to help you borrow some evidence before you leap:

 **Elaina Ray**

It's been two months since my breakup.

At first, it felt like one-hundred-foot monster waves crashing down on me every few seconds. I couldn't breathe through all the grief, waves tearing at and washing away the reality and the love I had known.

It went on like this for weeks and weeks until I could finally get a few minutes and hours between the sets.

Now they come once in a while, taking me by surprise and knocking me out for a bit, but overall, the feeling is more like a dull ache in my center, like a battered surfer dealing with an old injury as she tries to get back out in the ocean.

I realize I'll never not love René. It's a strange feeling to realize that this kind of love never goes away. I'm just making a 3D decision about what to make of the love and what to do with it, and we're consciously choosing not to use that love to be in a relationship.

It's weird. It's hard. But it's also comforting to know it's not going away. There will always be a divine connection between us. Now I have room for a new love and this friendship love too. More love, I tell myself. Room for more love. Tape that mantra to my mirror and try to tell myself it's real.

Because lately it feels like a total absence of love. A huge, long, dark void in my romantic life. No partner love. No Friday night "I don't feel like going out, let's curl up and watch a movie" love. No "someone I love in the seat next to me on the airplane" love. No default "I for sure will be held in the arms of a man I love today" love. No "I always know where he is" love. No "predictable, steady, honest, imperfect, sometimes kind of boring but also deep, rich, and familiar" love.

So, I hang in the void.

I'm working on my self-love.

I'm learning new feminine rituals.

Seeking out my sisters.

Dancing with my community.

Signing up for courses and retreats.

Getting to know myself again.

Raising my sexual consciousness.

Raising my spiritual consciousness.

Preparing myself to meet my next love.

But also, not preparing.

Not reaching. Not trying to make anything happen. Not seeking outward.

Sitting in the void. Listening to the lonely ache. Listening to the new desires as they slowly sprout up from the fresh soil of single life. Watching the petals of new parts of me slowly open.

Holding my heart in the waves when and if they come, days and weeks apart. Sitting on the edge of the shore, tender, and alive.

HOMEWORK FOR THIS CHAPTER

1. What is one area where you might be expecting yourself to change your mind or question your truth because it's an uncommon truth and makes you different from others around you? What would it be like to fully accept yourself and this truth as it is, right here, right now? What might become available to you then?

2. If you knew you couldn't mess it up or get it wrong because you fully trusted your path unfolding exactly as it's meant to for your greater good, always, then what is the one thing you would do right now?

3. A scary decision can really be a sign of where the aliveness lies for you. What would you do if you were committed to your raw aliveness?

4. From where and whom might you borrow evidence that truly all is well on the other side? Who takes huge leaps of faith and demonstrates success and confidence with their bold decision-making that inspires you? Use their stories to bolster your heart.

CHAPTER 17

THE ART OF RECEIVING MORE

LISBON, PORTUGAL
JANUARY 16, 2022

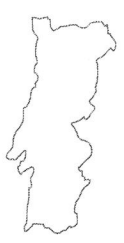

I sat across from an old friend of mine from college at a wine bar in the heart of Lisbon, the waiters serving us dinner in delightful Portuguese time, a lingering three-hour meal of tapas, bread, olives, fresh cheese, and everything served with lots of butter and olive oil. I was two weeks into the worst breakup of my life, and drowning my sorrows in trendy Mediterranean cuisine was becoming a favorite pastime.

But that night we were trying to figure out how to help my American friend manifest a highly sought-after permanent residency to the United Kingdom. She had already been rejected once and was reapplying with a new fervor, better recommendations, and more awareness of the seriousness of the application process.

The trouble was, as much effort as she was putting into the pursuit of a British visa, when I asked her if she really wanted to live in London or Lisbon, she just shrugged her shoulders and continued forking mushroom and date risotto onto her plate. She could go either way, she said. She had no clear pull; she knew she'd be happy either way.

What I saw was exactly the reason she got rejected in the first place. Murky, complacent energy. The universe couldn't deliver a miracle visa if she wasn't fully clear on her desire, aligned to her truth, and taking radical ownership of how much she was responsible for cocreating the outcome—and how badly she wanted it. Even if it looked like government bureaucrats would determine her fate, *she* actually did.

What I also saw was a reason why many people don't receive their wild, extraordinary, outlandish desires: fear of disappointment.

> YOU HAVE TO LEAVE MURKY ENERGY LAND, CRYSTALLIZE YOUR DESIRE AND POINT IT IN ONE DIRECTION, AND BE WILLING TO RISK FEELING HUGE AMOUNTS OF DISAPPOINTMENT BECAUSE OF THAT CLARITY AND OWNERSHIP OF YOUR TRUTH.
>
> YOU CAN ONLY BE MET BY THE THING YOU DESIRE WHEN YOU'RE FULLY BACKING YOUR TRUTH AND YOU'VE BREATHED ALL THE HOPE INTO YOUR INFLATABLE LIFE VEST.

Deep down, my friend badly wanted to be a Londoner. Lisbon wasn't a full-body yes for her, and nowhere else felt like home. At thirty-one, she felt out of control of the whole process, like she was drifting around the world, waiting to be cleared for landing so she could finally put down roots somewhere.

It felt much too risky to put her entire fate in this one basket, wanting it so badly, picturing herself there, lining up the jobs, looking at adorable East London flats, because what if it didn't work? The disappointment would be too enormous. It would be crippling. Better to stay nonchalant, hand over the power to the universe, and hide the potency of the true desire just a little out of reach for safekeeping so it doesn't shatter into a thousand pieces if it doesn't come true.

Sound familiar? People do this with financial aspirations, travel desires, job opportunities, love interests, and business ideas. Where are you doing this in your life right now? Where are you not admitting to yourself just how badly you want something because you're terribly afraid you can't have it, won't have it, or it'll fall through and your hopes that buoyed you up to the surface of life with so much aliveness will come crashing down and cut you open?

This is precisely the problem, paradox, and opportunity when it comes to receiving more in your life in terms of money, business opportunities, visibility, dating, and wild dreams of all kinds coming true. You have to leave murky energy land, crystallize your desire and point it in *one* direction, and be willing to risk feeling huge amounts of disappointment because of that clarity and ownership of your truth.

You can only be met by the thing you desire when you're fully backing your truth and you've breathed all the hope into your inflatable life vest. Bobbing along the surface of aliveness and vulnerability, there and only there do you have the chance for a miracle at your most tender edge.

Currently, I'm in the throes of disappointment of a flavor most people dread in their bones and that paralyzes dreams they don't even know they have. I'm sitting alone in a random apartment on the other side of the world away from my friends, community, home, pets, and partner, three weeks into a six-week trip that I was supposed to be on with my beloved. We had intended to go to the pyramids, snorkel in the Red Sea, walk through Paris together, and return to Bali hand in hand, memories made, partnership dreams fulfilled, and stronger than ever.

Instead, I'm picking up the pieces of my shattered heart. A ring sits in a tiny red box back in Bali, picked out by a man I'm deeply in love with, that I'll never wear.

It's the stuff of every little girl's worst nightmares. It could paralyze and scar me, crystallize bitterness into my cells, and hold my new, emerging desires hostage to "what if" scenarios and doubt, judgment, regret, fear, and skepticism.

Or it could crack me open, soften me, and empower me by the willingness I have to know and stand in my truth and ask for it. It could prove to the part of me and you that fears disappointment above all else that this fear, this mere *theory* that makes us turn away from the biggest and most important desires we have, simply doesn't hold up. Because we're built to sustain it. At the heart of our deepest disappointment, there's an important rebound mechanism, like a refueling station that only makes you more unfuckwithable.

What do I feel at the bottom of this particular disappointment? More strength.

What did I *choose to feel* at the bottom of getting fired, being rejected dozens of times on my first sales calls as I was trying to build my business, and every Valentine's Day for nine years while I was single? More hope and resolution. More clarity around the bigness and importance of my desires.

I chose to lock in that the belief of my desiring the things I desire means they are available to me and are, in fact, already on their way. Along what timeline, I couldn't know, but I can always hold onto the faith, find my strength at the bottom of every valley where my sacred refueling station lies, and continue taking the steps I know to take to follow the raw truth of those desires, the hands on my compass.

BECAUSE THE VERY POWER NECESSARY TO CREATE WHAT YOU WANT LIES IN THE SPECIFIC, RECKLESS, AND TOTALNESS OF CHOOSING IT, PLUS CLAIMING IT IN A WAY THAT RISKS EMOTIONAL SCARS, THE CRUMBLING OF DEARLY ENVISIONED TIMELINES, AND FACING EARTH-SHATTERING DISAPPOINTMENT.

So, ask yourself now in the quietness of your heart:

Where are you dulling down your desires, telling yourself you'll be fine with less, settling, and making do because you don't want to feel a sensation that not only are you built to survive but that also fills you with unexpected strength, clarity, hope, and all the unique ingredients for the next level of receivership of what's available and reserved specifically for you? Necessary ingredients for an extraordinary life of miracles and abundance that you can't actually get anywhere else.

Essentially, what is required for the level of extraordinary success you desire and know is meant for you is the ability to fly in the face of looming disappointment—a perceived den of darkness and despair that would prevent most people (but not you) from choosing their heart's deepest, craziest desire, and choosing it bigger with deep clarity, and choosing it with the risk of it not happening right away or in the way they imagine it or maybe ever at all.

Because *the very power necessary to create what you want* lies in the specific, reckless, and totalness of choosing it, plus claiming it in a way that risks emotional scars, the crumbling of dearly envisioned timelines, and facing earth-shattering disappointment.

So, what did I tell my dear Londoner-to-be friend in the tavern that night in Portugal, in her self-imposed purgatory of not admitting to herself what she really wanted, and thereby disenfranchising herself from the very power required to play her role in creating it?

Decide what you *really* want. Not "what you'd be okay with or what you'd make do with or settle for if it didn't work out because it's not likely to happen anyway" kind of a vibe, but what brings your heart alive. What do you truly feel called to have, do, be, and experience in this life? Claim that. Then act as if it's already done. Look at flats in London, imagine yourself living there, talk to your contacts and line up jobs, speak to me as if it's already a done deal, make plans in alignment with that reality and, most importantly, be with the longing for it to be true.

> WHEN YOU OCCUPY YOUR INNER LONGING SO COMPLETELY AND TAKE A DEEP PLUNGE INTO ITS RICH TEXTURE, YOU ENCOUNTER A FULLNESS OF NATURE AND HUMAN EXPERIENCE AND ALIVENESS THAT ERADICATES ALL SCARCITY. YOU MEET A FUNDAMENTALLY ABUNDANT ENERGY THAT RIPPLES OUT THROUGH YOU AND CONNECTS YOU TO THE VERY THING YOU LONG FOR AND PULLS IT CLOSER TO YOU ON YOUR TIMELINE. AT THE BOTTOM OF YOUR PAINFUL LONGING IS RAW POWER.

You, my dear reader, get to become intimate with your longing, which might feel uncomfortable or make you want to discharge it or despise it, but the creative power you have to exercise in the energetic fields of possibility all around you lies inside that longing. Sit with it, listen to it, move your body with it, pray with it, and allow it to be there, without trying to predict if it's right or wrong or going to come true or not. The longing itself is truth. It's real. It's inside of you, guiding you somewhere. It contains sorrow, depth, beauty, power, anger, and fullness.

On the surface, a longing can feel like scarcity, like you're missing something and there's an ache because it's not there. That surface-level interaction with your longing may well be what keeps the desire it points to away from you. When you occupy your inner longing so completely and take a deep plunge into its rich texture, you encounter a fullness of nature and human experience and aliveness that eradicates all scarcity. You meet a fundamentally abundant energy that ripples out through you and connects you to the very thing you long for and pulls it closer to you on your timeline. At the bottom of your painful longing is raw power. There's fullness, a fullness of longing.

Let me repeat that again and let your mind get wrapped around this concept one more time: When you fully occupy a longing for something that isn't yet here for you—which could otherwise feel like scarcity and thus create experiences from the energy of lack that don't look like what you long for—you are able to turn that sensation into a feeling of fullness, an abundant energy, which provides you positive energy for creation and attracting the very thing you desire. Essentially, if you feel lack in your longing, you attract lack. If you occupy your experience of longing and feel its fullness and abundance, you attract fullness and abundance.

Does this mean you get exactly what you long for in the exact shape and texture you imagined it in? No, of course not.

Does this mean you can accelerate timelines, widen the field of possibility, open up for miracles, and invite in outcomes that are closely related and maybe even exactly match your original desires by choosing to see it this way? Yes to all of that.

In the scorching pain of my heartbreak, I can choose to still occupy the longing I have for a soul-mate, lifetime partnership and focus the richness of that desire not on the lack of a partner in the present but on the total presence and complete fullness of my heart when I think of being met in the future in the way I desire. When I think of walking hand in hand with that man someday, I radiate joy, possibility, love, and peace.

> IF YOU OCCUPY YOUR EXPERIENCE OF LONGING AND FEEL ITS FULLNESS AND ABUNDANCE, YOU ATTRACT FULLNESS AND ABUNDANCE.

At the end of the day, as Wayne Dyer teaches, *you attract what you are, not what you want.* So become fullness, love, acceptance, wild possibility, abundance, care, and undying support for yourself and your desires. It doesn't mean you get all your desires, but it means you'll attract fullness, love, acceptance, wild possibility, abundance, care, and undying support in a myriad of unexpected and beautiful ways. Imagine what dreams and possibilities you can manifest from that space.

Here are some other secrets to wild receivership:

- **Clean out your energy pool of regret.** Regret interferes with your ability to receive and contributes to unconscious feelings of unworthiness and stuckness. As painful as some things from your past may have been, everything you've been through has got you to where you are now, right on time, right on purpose. Yes, even the most painful, harsh, and traumatic experiences. You get to choose to see that everything is happening for you and every choice you made has actually been perfect for the long-term alignment and path you're meant to be on. What is one mistake or regret you have in life that you could choose to see differently? I understand that it's not always easy to see it differently, but it's possible. And how would you think and feel if you chose to embrace that regret and move into acceptance, trust, and gratitude around it? With business, you can regret that you didn't start sooner, or you can regret an investment you made that looks like it didn't work out—or you could choose to see how it's all serving you in the bigger picture. Demoralizing self-criticism and radical self-support are both available to you at any time. Which one do you want to choose and how could that decision generate more momentum for you to receive more from life? Can you choose to see everything, even your mistakes, as forward movement? Giving yourself grace around your perceived mistakes also opens up huge amounts of freedom and increases your leadership potential. If you're afraid to mess up, you'll move through the world in a contracted and careful way, and if you make a mistake, your harsh self-criticism, much like a controlling parent, will come in and wag its finger at you, keeping you small. If you allow yourself the ability to make mistakes and trust yourself to make things right after you notice one, you'll not only be a better leader, but you'll also set the example for others that they don't have to be perfect and avoid making mistakes at all costs in order to be successful.

- **Faith as an exercise and a muscle.** You can't receive what you don't believe you can have, so practice having more faith in being able to have what you say you want to receive. The people I see who stay stuck the longest or block themselves from receiving are looking out into the world for evidence around them that what they desire is out there and realistically making its way toward them. The people who I see tap into their magic and pursue their most beautiful, wildly successful timelines are people who close their eyes, see what they see inside themselves, listen to what actions they are guided to take, and keep moving forward . . . until one day they look up and see the thing they once only saw in the wispy, tear-streaked vision of their hidden kingdom.

- **Act in spite of no evidence.** If you want to receive more than you ever have before (money, clients, love, visibility, opportunities), then you cannot wait for external evidence to preapprove you and deem you worthy and fitting of a level of attention, leadership, and financial success you simply haven't seen before. You're going to need to act before you see that it's locked in or that a certain outcome is guaranteed. Choose to put your prices up, invest in something scary, leave a relationship, tell someone you love them, reach out to a potential collaborator, ask for the stage, and do something you don't feel worthy of. You do it first and *then* you will see the evidence and get the feedback that you were meant to do it. Then your true embodied feelings of confidence and worthiness grow within you. Then you can use that newfound confidence to lean into something else you don't feel 100 percent ready for and repeat and reinforce this muscle that allows you to receive more in your life than if you waited for "permission" to do what you simply felt guided to do in the first place.

- **Follow your aliveness.** A great prompt to ask yourself and to start noticing in your day-to-day life is: What makes me come alive? Allow your curiosity to guide you. You're meant to receive more of what fills you with life-force energy. It's a good indicator of alignment, and your timeline of maximum fulfillment and abundance will arise by pursuing what makes you come alive.

- **Community.** I know I got to where I am today by surrounding myself with more and more inspiring people—people who have made me a better human, people who have inspired and supported me, and people who model what I want to have, do, be, and receive. You are truly the average of who you surround yourself with, so how can you put yourself in environments with the people you aspire to be like, virtually or in the flesh? I moved to Bali because I wanted to be around successful digital nomads who were able to live full time on a tropical island so that I could learn to do the same.

> FEEL FULL AND TAKEN CARE OF NOW AND YOU'LL CONTINUE TO MANIFEST EXPERIENCES THAT STRENGTHEN AND DEEPEN THAT FEELING. FEEL LACK AND INSUFFICIENCY NOW AND YOU'LL CONTINUE TO MANIFEST EXPERIENCES THAT AMPLIFY THAT FEELING BACK TO YOU TOO. THE CHOICE IS YOURS.

- **Gratitude and digestion.** I first heard of this concept from Mama Gena, and it really took gratitude practices to a new level for me. You cannot receive more if you haven't fully digested the beauty and support and richness you already have in your life. It's like trying to eat more cake but your mouth is completely full because you haven't swallowed what you already have. You're a match for more abundance when you feel abundant now. Look around and appreciate the home you have, the car you're driving, every dollar that's in your bank account right now. Feel full and taken care of now and you'll continue to manifest experiences that strengthen and deepen that feeling. Feel lack and insufficiency now and you'll continue to manifest experiences that amplify that feeling back to you too. The choice is yours.

- **Your radical truth will bring you the greatest abundance.** Repeat the next few lines, save them to your phone, write them on a sticky note, or do what you need to do to remember them:

    When I am in my truth,
    When I am living as I'm meant to be living,
    When I'm showing up fully as the person I am meant to be,
    When I'm pursuing growth for the sake of my growth,
    When I'm fully in the flow of my genius and purpose,
    I open myself up to receiving more.

HOMEWORK FOR THIS CHAPTER

1. Make a desires list. Take out a piece of paper and write down a list of fifty things you desire. Get in the habit of being in touch with what you really want, no matter how big or trivial what comes to mind may seem. Wanting to start a nonprofit organization to provide affordable housing in your hometown is just as valuable and worthy as wanting to eat chocolate chip cookie dough out of the tube like you did as a kid or buy a fancy pair of sunglasses. Make a list every Monday for a month and watch how many desires you start to bring to reality that were buried in busyness or ignorance.

2. Down with denial. What are three desires from the list that you haven't fully owned up to because the disappointment if you didn't receive them would feel big and potentially crippling? Are you finally willing to risk facing disappointment in order to have these dreams come true?

3. Transmute your longing. Set aside time to be with the bodily sensations that arise from not having the money, lover, body, success, or other major part of your life you want to have in place that simply isn't in place yet. Feel the fiery burn of the anger in your stomach, feel the contraction in your

throat, feel the ache in your heart, feel the sexual aliveness course through your veins or your womb with nowhere to go. Can you fully occupy your body and merge with those sensations? Can you stay with the feelings and discomfort long enough to feel the raw power emerge at your core? Sway your body with the power, stomp your feet, beat your hands into a pillow, scream out loud, or melt into a near orgasmic ecstasy as you tap into that smoldering sensation well below the surface. Do this activity on a daily basis, just five or ten minutes at a time, and watch your life change. Watch the things you long for begin to manifest when you stop turning away the literal and physical sensations of your very longing for them.

4. Create space to receive. Where can you actually create more space for what you want to receive? If you want more clients, how can you clear your calendar so you have time to take them on? If you want a partner, how can you put a date night on your calendar every week and take yourself out the way you'd want a man to show up and romance you? If you want more passion, how can you create passionate self-pleasure rituals every week until your lover manifests? If you want more money, how can you clean out your wallet, tidy up your accounting statements, and hire a wealth adviser to create space for more financial abundance?

5. Forgiveness and cleaning up past regrets. What are you going to forgive yourself for right now and move forward?

CHAPTER 18

LOCKING IN CONSISTENCY IN YOUR BUSINESS

LISBON, PORTUGAL
JANUARY 20, 2022

Consistency is one of the most seemingly mysterious elements of being an entrepreneur, and one of the most desirable results for many business owners, which probably includes you. You want to be able to do your own thing, make your own schedule, be your own boss, influence the internet, put out amazing products and services you love, and work with your choice of clients, and wouldn't it be nice if the money was just as consistent as the good ol' paycheck days, but just a lot *more*?

I'm here to let you in on a little secret: Consistency is not something outside of your control, leaving you merely subject to the whims and waves of the market and external forces. You are very much in control when it comes to consistency, and that's what I'm going to teach you in this chapter.

You can actually plan for it, put systems in place to create it, and set **yourself up to expect it.** The funny little trick is that the higher your threshold and tolerance to face inconsistency and keep going anyway, and the greater willingness you have to weather the ups and downs of being in business, the more consistent you're likely to be.

This means that should you have a low month or a flopped launch, the less likely you are to make it mean something about who you are or create a story around it—and the more consistent you'll wind up being. The bigger deal you make out of fluctuating income, the clingier and more attached you are to specific numbers and results, and the more entrenched your stories are about what you need in order to feel good or safe as an entrepreneur, the more your desired results will consistently hold themselves just out of your reach until you look more closely at those parts of yourself.

If you can be committed to your vision regardless of the timeline or the tribulations required to achieve it, then you'll find success comes easily and swiftly to you because there's no other energetic interference or unnecessary resistance since you're already all in, for as long as it takes, no matter what. Results love that vibe.

> YOU DECIDE THAT YOU'RE CERTAIN AND SECURE AND COMMITTED AND ALL-IN ON YOUR VISION, THEN THE WORLD REARRANGES ITSELF TO MATCH THAT INTERNALLY ANCHORED DECISION YOU ARE HOLDING WITHIN YOU.

Let's start with the energetic pieces here and then go into covering the practical business decisions and systems you'll get to set up to provide consistency.

Consistency, first of all, starts with embracing the process instead of getting wrapped up in very fixed ideas of the results you need to see in order to feel the journey is worthwhile or that you're on track or reassured to be imminently successful. That feeling of certainty and security cannot come from external evidence or outside validation, as we've covered elsewhere in the book, it comes from inside. You decide that you're certain and secure and committed and all-in on your vision, then the world rearranges itself to match that internally anchored decision you are holding within you.

The energetic decision is powerful. When clients come to me struggling with consistency, I'll have them examine other areas of their life outside of business and do a checkup on where they are and are not holding the energy of consistency, commitment, and follow-through.

Energetic Tune-Up

Identify your energy leaks. Let's do this together right now.
In your life:
- Are you being consistent in your diet and exercise?
- Are you consistent in upholding your boundaries and desires in the dating scene?
- Are you being consistent in your friendships and community life, showing up when your loved ones need you?
- Are you always late to everything or canceling at the last minute?
- Are you consistent in saving and investing money?
- Are you staying committed to yourself and your principles in the romantic partnership(s) you're in?

These are some places to start looking for leaks and cleaning up your energy.

Any behavior that exhibits wobbliness or wishy-washiness is going to show up in your business, like it or not, regardless of whether it's directly related to the business.

It's about your energetic signature in the world, formed through your thoughts, feelings, and actions in all parts of your life, and it will magnetize and create situations that are a match for that.

Now, let's put that same microscopic lens over the business:

- Are you leading and going first?
- Are you consistently talking about your work and letting people know who you are and what you offer?
- Are you committed to showing up and selling every day so the people who want what you have to offer can easily find you and pay you?
- Are you consistent in showing up and delivering excellence to your existing clients?
- Are you continuously doing your market research and creating strong programs that people want to buy?
- Are you committed to talking to your people and building genuine relationships with them, regardless of whether they do anything for you in return, like buy your stuff, like your posts, share your posts, etc.?

Consistency starts with you. You don't wait to see certain levels of results before you show up like a true professional. True professionals are the ones who get paid lots of money, consistently, by people who love their work and love to pay them. But you have to get yourself into that professional mindset first, even if your business feels like a side hustle or an inspirational Instagram hobby right now. You lead by acting as if you already have the results you desire and move from that place of certainty in who you are and where you're going before you see any evidence of it occurring.

One last piece intertwined with consistency is **availability**. I'm simply not available to *not* show up consistently in my business, no matter what is happening in my personal life. It's the same feeling as how I'm not available to go into debt, get drunk, or eat large amounts of gluten or meat. These are just things I'd never do or tolerate in my life anymore, so they don't happen. It's a combination of a standard I set for these things not to occur and a deep understanding of nonnegotiable values I hold.

For example, when I broke up with my partner and was left stranded in Europe, bouncing around countries and time zones for a month (which was only a few weeks ago in real time as I'm writing this and is, in fact, still going on as I commit to getting my book done on time), I had to recommit to *my commitment* to commitment.

Everything I preach about consistency in business is being tested as we speak, so I'm sharing this with you from a deepened and embodied understanding of what's required to realistically achieve this level of success as a human who goes through all the typical ups and downs of being alive—heartbreak, health issues, deaths in the family, unexpected relocations, emotional distress—and still wants to be an entrepreneur whose business is thriving. You get to have both. You don't have to choose. But you do have to bring yourself back to the decision to be committed again and again.

> CONSISTENCY STARTS WITH YOU. YOU DON'T WAIT TO SEE CERTAIN LEVELS OF RESULTS BEFORE YOU SHOW UP LIKE A TRUE PROFESSIONAL.

For the past month, I've been writing content on my laptop balanced on my knees at various boarding gates throughout Europe, typing frantically before my boarding zone is called. I've been burying my head into the seat in front of me on the plane anytime I think about my former partner and God forbid look at my phone and see Facebook reminding me that I was curled up in his arms in the Komodo Islands exactly one year ago. I've been taking PCR tests, going to government agencies to get travel papers, and rebooking flights based on changing COVID restrictions. I've been holding client calls in the airport lounges between flights. I've had my team cancel and rearrange meetings sometimes up to three or four times because I changed time zones and got double-booked somehow. I've been eating croissants and cheese and chicken when I'd normally never touch any of that, adapting my tendency to be on a strict eating regime to the realities of continental Europe. There's been no kind of routine, completely nonideal circumstances all around, I'm separated from my friends and community in Bali, and now my beloved of two and a half years is gone.

> THE TRUTH IS, WHEN YOU CREATE A BUSINESS YOU LOVE, IT'S NOT HARD TO SHOW UP. IN FACT, IT WOULD BE HARD NOT TO.

Let's be honest. It's been a shit show. Totally nonideal in every way.

And all that said, I've not missed any of my client calls. I'm finishing the first draft of this book by the deadline. I had a successful course launch and new enrollments in all my high-level programs as well. Our marketing presence hasn't suffered in the slightest. In fact, I've been feeling more inspired and creative due to the high emotions and intense healing process I'm currently in, and I've chosen to share parts of it with my audience, bringing us into an even deeper connection. I had 400 people sign up for a masterclass I put out at the beginning of the month, I was featured on a huge international online summit, and we're closing out January 2022 with another $100,000 in revenue. Consistent.

This is not because I pushed myself, sacrificed myself, or ignored my emotions. Quite the opposite. It's a reflection of the fact that I have a business that is a healthy separate entity that runs like a machine, regardless of how I feel. I was able to tend to myself, make the best of my hectic personal situation, and heal my heartbreak while the company operated in a state of being calm, cool, business as usual.

This isn't a coincidence or sheer luck. I've built it intentionally so my business supports *me* first and foremost and the life I want to have. I want to be a human who travels, has things get messy, gets her heart broken, does crazy shit, and lives for the adventure of the fullness of life. I'm flying out to the Maldives in a few days to work on this book while sitting in front of the most pristine ocean and sand on the planet, checking in with my team between snorkels, and putting any calls on hold until I feel sufficiently suntanned and spoiled by my inner masculine who is coming out to take care of me as I open this new chapter of my life.

This is all available to me because I've chosen to create it step by step with this intention. As long as I have Wi-Fi and my phone, I can fundamentally be anywhere under any circumstances and the business will stay afloat. I regularly take time off-line and away from social media for complete detoxes and the business still runs and makes six-figure months without my direct oversight. No micromanaging required.

The truth is, when you create a business you love, it's not hard to show up. In fact, it would be hard *not to*.

There's no push to do it anyway, or to roll out of bed and be something I'm not, or to overextend myself or sacrifice myself . . . it's the exact opposite. The work I do has a natural rhythm to it, it involves people I've hand-selected to be in my space, and it involves doing things I couldn't stop doing if I tried. It's my purpose.

I work just two to three hours per day. I have things set up so I have a team of support behind the scenes to keep things running. I have very few live calls, and I have the flexibility as CEO to move anything around whenever I need to—so my business works with me and my life and desires, not against me.

It's the ultimate blessing that comes with choosing to become self-made and run your own business.

I am so grateful I chose this long ago because my business supports me to have the time for grief, personal development, fun, challenge, healing, and any of the other ups and downs. It's not an impediment to anything I want or need to do, but it supports me in everything I want and need to do.

Work doesn't feel like a burden. It's an effortless extension of my heart and what excites me and brings me joy.

My alignment check on my business and life is clear: Even in my darkest hours, my purpose shines bright. My work is my cure. My portal for deep healing, expansion, creativity, and life-changing impact.

I write the social media posts I write at the length and volume I write them at because I *need* to get them out on the page because it feels good to me to share (that it changes other people's lives is a secondary happy ripple effect).

I get on livestream because I feel turned on about talking about what I'm talking about, and I can't *not* share. It would cost me too much to hold it in.

I follow my highest excitement and trust that the spillover vibration of me doing that and trusting myself and what lights me up also lights up the others around me who are meant to be touched by my work.

I create programs because I feel excited about bringing people together and getting to know amazing, top-level entrepreneurs and the rising stars of this industry. It's fun for me. It also most definitely helps the people who choose to be there.

> PEOPLE ASK ME WHAT THE SECRET TO MY PROLIFIC CREATION AND CONSISTENCY IS . . . AND THIS IS IT. I DO IT FOR ME AND MY PURPOSE AND JOY. I DON'T TRY TO SAVE YOU WITH OR CATER TO YOUR NEEDS (OR LIMITATIONS), I JUST LET OUT WHAT NEEDS TO BE LET OUT. BECAUSE IT SAVES ME. IT BRINGS ME ALIVE.

This has been the energy I've been in since I started writing and sharing online over a decade ago. I get a ridiculous amount of stuff done in just a few hours per day in insanely effective ways. I have produced a *prolific* amount of content and have no intention of stopping or drying up. I wrote this book in just four months.

My content has changed thousands of people's lives and turned many ordinary humans into millionaire business owners. The methodologies and structures I've developed have been used by tens of thousands of others who teach them now as well—because I coached their coach, and they got into the "lineage" whether they know it or not.

None of this comes from me slaving away over my business, all hunched over, doing things for other people and "pretzeling" myself up to cater to other people's needs or expectations or forcing myself to pump out content and sales. If I wanted to do that, I'd have stayed at IBM as a financial consultant and continued to work for someone else.

My results, my lifestyle, and my impact all stem from knowing and deciding that my work gets to be massively successful and of high service because I follow the inspiration and creative energy coming naturally through me. It came as a result of opening the floodgates on my desires and doing what I can't help but do because it's who I am.

People ask me what the secret to my prolific creation and consistency is . . . and this is it. I do it for me and my purpose and joy. I don't try to save you with or cater to your needs (or limitations), I just let out what needs to be let out. Because it saves me. It brings me alive.

This is what I help rearrange and untangle with my highest-level clients who may have forgotten that this simple and organic way to run a very successful business (and reach lots of people) exists by working with your God-given gifts and effervescence.

Let me break down exactly what components of my business help me do this so you can create this same reality if you desire it as well. To me, there are two key principles that have helped me become self-made and consistent:

1. **I am not my business**. It is a completely separate entity from me, even though as a personal brand, I am the face and voice of the

company. When I first started my business, I did everything, like most entrepreneurs who are just starting up. I was the accountant, the marketing manager, the sales team, the CEO, the copywriter, the secretary, the media relations team, and the web developer. If I didn't show up to work, nothing got done because nothing existed outside of what I personally was able to think up, create, and deliver. Now, I have other people to think up ideas, deliver services to the clients, execute on plans, and represent the company to the outside world. There's a mission that's bigger than just "pay Elaina's rent in Bali." There are more forces at play and more people who care about our work than just me. Other people have my back, and it's one of the best feelings in the world.

2. **The irony of becoming self-made is that you don't get there on your own.** I have a COO, a marketing manager, a graphic designer, a podcast producer, a web developer, two support coaches, and a sales lead. None of this is hard to manage or is overwhelming because I brought them on one step at a time and I know the truth: The more help I hire, the more money I make. The more I delegate, the more value I generate. The more hands we have on deck, the more people we are able to serve.

> THE MORE HELP I HIRE, THE MORE MONEY I MAKE. THE MORE I DELEGATE, THE MORE VALUE I GENERATE. THE MORE HANDS WE HAVE ON DECK, THE MORE PEOPLE WE ARE ABLE TO SERVE.

Besides putting a team into place, here are the six core things that go into making your business a consistent machine of service and profitability:

- **Automated lead generation and nurturing.** Even if I stopped posting inspired "live" content on social media like I do today (ahem, the team does so with preplanning and prescheduling) every day, I'd still be attracting new people, welcoming them into my world, serving them with free and paid content, and warming them up to see whether they want to work together. People I've never heard of consistently book calls for exploring mastermind and private coaching with our sales team due to these systems.

CLASSIC MARKETING WISDOM: IT'S EASIER AND CHEAPER TO KEEP A CUSTOMER THAN TO ACQUIRE A NEW ONE.

- **Systematized launches.** Launching is no big deal. We are always selling because we are a business. From the moment of inspiration when I go "I want to offer THIS next!" (which is my primary job as CEO), we have a fixed way of going about it—the steps that need to occur are documented and everyone knows what part they play. This allows me to pretty much come up with the idea then deliver it, staying in my zone of genius as creator, visionary, and coach.

- **Structured signature product suite with natural client ascension.** Clients in my world consistently re-enroll in programs where they are seeing great results and/or move up to the next offer where we work in more advanced stages of their business. This makes sales even easier because people who are working well with us just opt to stay in our world. Classic marketing wisdom: It's easier and cheaper to keep a customer than to acquire a new one.

- **Recurring monthly revenue.** I have several long-term programs with payment plans and naturally, a percentage of our clients choose those, which brings in a solid chunk of predictable recurring revenue every month.

- **Support coaches to help support on delivery.** It's a game changer to not be the only one supporting my clients' transformation. I have specialist coaches who I've trained and who have their own areas of expertise who assist my clients with things like copywriting, operations, hiring, mindset work, and social media strategy.

- **Leveraged offers with mostly group coaching.** This isn't for everyone, it just personally works well for me and my business model. I have very few calls and fixed appointments per week, like three or four tops, which gives me loads of free time to be in the CEO visionary seat of the business and doing other zone-of-genius work while actually giving more people access to my magic and the magic of my team.

To summarize, consistency is an inside job. It's something you have full control over creating on both an energetic and strategic plane. It's not a magical force or universal blessing that will either be bestowed on you by the gods or not, it's actually something you can predictably generate. You simply implement one system at a time, one step at a time, and one day at a time, preferably alongside someone who has done this before and can show you the way. When you have a business that's a healthy separate entity running on its own and supporting *you*, rather than you running ragged to support it, you'll be able to weather any of the natural ups and downs that come with being human as well as a self-made CEO.

HOMEWORK FOR THIS CHAPTER

1. Name three concrete steps you could take based on inspiration from this chapter to create more consistency in your business and revenue today.

2. How can you create a healthier separation between you and your business? Who do you need to hire? Do you resonate with the idea of expanding your team or implementing more automations? Or do you need to befriend the mindset and get used to the idea that you can be the voice of your personal brand, but that you are not the company itself? This may still be a new concept you're playing around with, but what does it mean and look like to you with your current understanding?

3. When personal life trials and tribulations occurred for you in the past, how was the business affected? Did you manage to stay consistent and lean into the support of your team or your mindset around professionalism and showing up, or did some of the balls get dropped? What could increase the resiliency of your business so you as the person behind the business have more freedom to have the full range of your human experience without it compromising and affecting your work?

4. What would an ideal workday and work week look and feel like? What can you realistically commit to doing consistently without overextending or overpromising?

5. Does your day-to-day have space for creativity, being (instead of doing), and play? Or do you find yourself running on fumes, uninspired to show up because you haven't had a moment to simply be? What are some ways you can create space in your day for yourself—or to work ON your business as the visionary instead of IN your business as the admin and delivery?

6. Your content. What feels natural to you—writing, livestreams, podcasts? Which platform(s) do you have the most fun showing up on? Focus on those places to be showing up consistently while your team plans and executes a content strategy to amplify your visibility on the other ones for you. Remember, *your business* can be visible through content repurposing and strategic scheduling while you, the human, are living your fullest life off-line.

CHAPTER 19

BUSTING MYTHS AND STORIES PEOPLE TELL ABOUT BUSINESS THAT JUST AREN'T TRUE

JAKARTA, INDONESIA
FEBRUARY 3, 2022

In the nearly seven years I've been coaching (at the time of writing), I've heard a lot of crazy stories that even really smart people tell themselves about business, money, and their own potential. And I've heard a lot of the *same* crazy stories over and over again from *lots* of smart people, so it seems a few of these are particularly insidious and apparently very common among entrepreneurs.

Are you currently telling yourself any of these? If so, rest assured that this is perfectly normal and lots of other highly capable people like you have these thoughts. However, it doesn't make them true, and it doesn't mean that these fears, doubts, or stories have the final say about what's in store for you.

Here's what I would tell you if you were sitting across from me in my office in Bali bringing me this crazy talk. Let's clear it up right now.

MYTH #1: I'm multi-passionate and can't pick one thing to focus my business on. That's why it's so hard for me to get started and find clients.

I hear you, Renaissance Man/Woman. You love healing, art, fashion, outdoor adventure, spirituality, business, health and cleansing, and the occasional foray into telling love stories and inspiring the world to have better relationships. I would consider myself a kindred soul who also takes interest and delight in so many of life's riches. I know I could run a very successful business in any of those categories, in fact.

But if I'm going to be honest with you, I've never met someone who was *uni-passionate*. Not a single one of my hundreds of clients has ever *not* described themselves as multi-passionate. I think it's actually called being human and containing multitudes. We have so many facets and layers to who we are: what excites us, fascinates us, inspires us, and moves us, so of course we are all multi-passionate, multidimensional beings. You are not unique for being multi-passionate. If you're human, you are multidimensional.

This is where I have to break your ego and point out your attachment to something I refer to as "specialness," which gets in the way of you and the rest of your life—the best things in life, in fact.

Specialness syndrome has you believe that there's some unique way you are blocked or some unique background or challenge that is so uncommon that it justifies why you don't have the thing you say you want. Essentially, you'd rather be right about your story than wrong and have the thing you want. How about you play to win instead? How about you focus on being right about being able to have the thing you actually want?

This whole syndrome is about justification and ultimately gives you the payoff of staying safe and comfortable by being more committed to your reasons for being stuck than to doing the damn thing no matter what. It's very common, even among smart overachievers, and it's easily surmountable. Having me put words to it and call it forward is enough for you to say, "Got it. Enough is enough. Let me prove my story wrong now. Let me be ordinary and just apply myself like everyone else who's ever become an entrepreneur has done and get the same results that are obviously readily available to anyone who chooses to be committed to their dreams instead of their stories."

The sooner you realize that most successful entrepreneurs specializing in one thing are actually multidimensional beings like you, the sooner you will be able to get out of your own way. They have simply made a smart decision to move in one direction of their liking so they can get established in the market and see revenue coming in. They know they are free to change at any time. They know they'll be more successful if they pick one thing and stick to it for a while.

My advice on niching? Do not wait for an epiphany or try to do a lot of healing work to find your purpose or wait until it dawns on you in some highly specific, somatic way where your guides and angels sing out and you get full-body orgasms telling you, "This is your niche." That is very unlikely to happen. What you'll need to do is unceremoniously choose something you like, perhaps not even that much more than all the other things you like, make a commitment to it, and run with it. You'll evolve, shift, pivot, and tweak along the way, so there's no need for it to be a perfect fit at the start either. It's *just* a starting point.

There's also no magic-pill coaching program or divine initiation that takes place where someone smarter than you can bestow your niche upon you because it just so happened to be lurking in a place within you that you can't see. It really boils down to this: Find a problem you can solve, pick something that people want—something that you would like to create and deliver—and start providing it to them. Business is quite that simple. Entrepreneurship is, in a nutshell, problem-solving at its finest. Entrepreneurs find ways to streamline, create, innovate, educate, and motivate the people around them every single day. Successful entrepreneurs are not only passionate about what they do, but they allow themselves to follow their visions, no matter how insane they might seem to those around them. Every creation, tool, system, brand, thing we have today was a result of someone's incredulous belief in themselves and the solution they felt called to provide.

My other piece of advice around this is that your audience is smart if you choose to view them as smart. They can understand that you primarily do one thing but also care about a variety of other topics. You can include more of you than just the niche product or service you're selling in your brand. You can share about your children, exotic travels, lessons in romance, art, and/or political views, should you desire. In my business, I am known for my coaching and marketing expertise and a lot of my content speaks about that, but I also share plenty about my world travels, home, relationship, cats, fashion, and health experiments (there's even an entire chapter in this book devoted to health, which is not my niche but is a big part of who I am). I choose to view my audience as perfectly capable of understanding that I'm a business coach *and* a woman who loves Bali, animals, real estate, love, and personal growth, among other things.

Let the fear go that the fullness of you can't come through the business because you choose to provide a niche service. It's actually quite

> LET THE FEAR GO THAT THE FULLNESS OF YOU CAN'T COME THROUGH THE BUSINESS BECAUSE YOU CHOOSE TO PROVIDE A NICHE SERVICE.

the opposite. You can primarily be known for one thing that serves one type of person, but you also need to bring your essence and multifaceted interests and energy through. Those are the exact reasons why people will choose to buy that thing from *you*. Many people hire me out of the sea of many thousands of business coaches because they know they'll get results with me *and* they love how much I love kirtan, or that I live in Bali, or that I have a healthy, spiritual relationship alongside my business success.

MYTH #2: I'm not a business coach and don't help my clients make money. I don't think I can ever be as successful in business because the results my clients get are more on the spiritual level, are more esoteric, intangible, and perhaps not even as highly valued as concrete financial increases.

Welcome to one of the most common stories I hear, and slay, every single day. First of all, most of the men and women I work with are not business coaches or teach about money the way I do. They come to me because that's my area of expertise, and they want to learn the skills and apply it to their businesses and purposes, most of which involve personal development, healing work, thought leadership, relationship coaching, spiritual guidance, and more. And they make lots and lots of money doing what they were put on this earth to do. They don't make lots and lots of money because they parrot my business model or use my messaging or do anything besides what they know they are supposed to do. You can borrow the evidence from the testimonials page of my website and from the thousands of millionaires running all different types of businesses until you're able to see this evidence for yourself.

> MONEY DOESN'T RESPOND TO ONE KIND OF MESSAGE OR PRODUCT, AND PEOPLE DON'T WANT JUST ONE TYPE OF TRANSFORMATION. MONEY RESPONDS TO YOU BEING IN ALIGNMENT WITH YOUR TRUTH AND DOING THE EXACT WORK YOU'RE MEANT TO BE DOING, AND PEOPLE WANT LOTS OF KINDS OF TRANSFORMATION.

The truth is, money doesn't respond to one kind of message or product, and people don't want just one type of transformation. Money responds to you being in alignment with your truth and doing the exact work you're meant to be doing, and people want lots of kinds of transformation. People want all the transformation, in fact. People want amazing health, transcendental sex, delicious relationships, thriving businesses, happy souls, healed hearts, finished books, clear purposes, and legacies they'll love to leave behind. Different people want different things, and they are all equally valuable. It's about connecting with the people who highly value the thing *you* do best.

Here's the thing you have to realize when you tell this particular story: You,

> IT'S ABOUT CONNECTING WITH THE PEOPLE WHO HIGHLY VALUE THE THING YOU DO BEST.

my love, are projecting. You are likely someone who is heavily invested in improving your skill set around business, becoming a thriving entrepreneur, and upleveling your relationship to money. After all, you downloaded this book or pulled it off the shelf. This is an area of focus for you. You may even be investing in coaches and programs and stretching what you believe is possible by putting yourself in rooms like my mastermind or other similar mentorship opportunities to help you achieve these results faster and easier. This is great—and this also creates your blind spot. You might very well believe that simply because this is an area of focus and earnest investment for you and many of the peers you may be surrounding yourself with that all other people desire the same, and if you don't provide the particular transformation that you've been seeking out and researching like crazy that you are less than or will underperform in your business. Simply not the case.

You've just forgotten about all the many people for whom money and business is of little interest. They have stable jobs, don't desire to be an entrepreneur and think you're awesome but crazy, or are already established business owners themselves who are facing other life challenges that keep them up at night: mysterious health issues, insidious anxiety or unhappiness, a lack of life partner, disconnection from their bodies and pleasure, recurring relationship patterns that make them want to pull their hair out, and dozens of other highly valuable problems that people like you probably solve. This is their number one area of focus. They, right now, are scouring the internet reading about healing, subconscious repatterning, yoga, cleansing, tantra, embodiment, and the like, hoping to come across someone with a clue about how they can evolve past their current issue, someone they can look up to in that particular area and say, "Wow, she really glows. She's figured this piece out. I need this medicine."

Your job is to own your truth and what you're here to work on with people, to be easy to find and identify as the solver of this problem, and to be an all-around obvious choice when they come across you as someone with authority, life experience, and embodied wisdom on this topic.

MYTH #3: I'm from such-and-such country and coaching and investing in the way you talk about is not common. I worry I have to lower my prices to match the market.

I've worked with people from dozens of countries on every single continent and have heard this story more times than I can count from clients who later go on to make unprecedented money in their niche and geography because I told them what I'm about to tell you and they chose to listen.

My answer can be summarized very succinctly: Make the choice to lead and not follow the market. Fuck the market. There's always room for brilliance, there's always room for a luxurious, high value, and distinguished offer, and there are always people who will choose to pay for the highest quality product or service they can find or choose to spend more because they deeply resonate with the person or brand they feel attracted to. Regardless of the

> MAKE THE CHOICE TO LEAD AND NOT FOLLOW THE MARKET. FUCK THE MARKET.

median income of your country, there will always be a select group of people who will have more resources and/or choose to allocate their resources differently than their peers, especially when there's a compelling offer.

Secondly, coaching is a multibillion-dollar industry that's booming. It's spreading into every single corner of the planet, and if it's not yet widely understood in your part of the world, it will be soon enough. Until then, you have two things going for you: You can position yourself in the international market and charge top dollar—*and* you get to be an early mover and trendsetter in your country. That way, when people start to seek out services in your niche in your part of the world, you'll be the OG who's been doing it the longest.

That reality is available to you. But so is the reality of dropping your prices and competing for the clients who have a scarcity mindset in one narrow part of the market, which becomes a race to the bottom instead of using a strategy to set yourself apart. Which position do you want to occupy?

MYTH #4: I want to be accessible to more people and don't want to sell higher priced programs because they won't be affordable to my audience.

You can charge whatever you want and build your business however you want. I'm not here to convince you to charge more. My clients come to me when they've tried this aforementioned path and later feel overworked and undervalued and resentful of their low-paying clients and are really done underselling themselves. When you get to that point, your prices will naturally elevate or you'll be ready to work with a coach to help support you in adjusting your business model to prioritize your well-being, and by prioritizing your energy and wellness, you'll be thus better serving the people you're meant to be serving.

You can either wait until that happens and then raise your rates or you can decide you're not even going to put yourself through that early entrepreneur stage of hell and simply charge what feels very nourishing to you from the beginning and position your brand well in the market from the beginning. Chanel didn't get to be Chanel by selling cheap purses and then incrementally raising her prices. She sold the divine, luxurious items of high value that she was called to make right from the beginning. What do you know your work to be?

Anchor into any pricing decision based on *you*, not based on external factors like what you think people can "afford" because affordability is not a fact—it's not measurable, it's not a set price range, it's a reflection of a person's mindset and it is assessed differently by everyone. The fact is that there's someone ready to buy at any price point, so you simply need to choose the prices that work best for you, not make your decisions based off projecting parts of your own scarcity mindset onto others and trying to twist your business into a pretzel to please others (or your assumptions of what others want and need). That has a flavor of codependency, not business leadership. Leaders decide what works for them and their businesses and let the

> THE FACT IS THAT THERE'S SOMEONE READY TO BUY AT ANY PRICE POINT, SO YOU SIMPLY NEED TO CHOOSE THE PRICES THAT WORK BEST FOR YOU.

market choose whether to buy from them or someone else and let everyone flow to purchase what works best based on their own needs and desires.

> ESTABLISH YOURSELF WITH A SUSTAINABLE, PROFITABLE BUSINESS MODEL SO YOU DON'T EVER HAVE TO WORRY ABOUT MEETING YOUR EXPENSES. WHEN YOU HAVE HIGH RECURRING REVENUE AND LOTS OF STABILITY, THEN HIRE A TEAM, PAY FOR THE ADS, WRITE THE BOOK, DO FREE WEBINARS, GIVE STUFF AWAY, DO LOW-COST OFFERS, LITERALLY DO WHATEVER YOU WANT THAT ALLOWS YOUR WORK TO BE ACCESSIBLE.

Pricing aside, let's talk about this "accessibility" piece. What I want to do is invite you into a longer-term perspective. You want to reach lots of people with your work, and that's beautiful. And you're going to be so much better equipped to do that with a lot more resources behind you. My recommendation? Establish yourself with a sustainable, profitable business model so you don't ever have to worry about meeting your expenses. When you have high recurring revenue and lots of stability, then hire a team, pay for the ads, write the book, do free webinars, give stuff away, do low-cost offers, literally do whatever you want that allows your work to be accessible. When you have the money to hire the book agency, run the ads, and pay your team, you'll reach more people effortlessly, from overflow. Not by thinking you're doing everyone a lot of favors by only charging $200 for a group program and trying to get 100 people into it every month to make ends meet. Being in scraping-by energy is not magnetic, not good for your well-being, and not the highest possible arrangement of service and compensation that is available to you.

What is available, however, is you being very well taken care of by serving just a handful of your most ready-to-invest, high-caliber customers (should oxygen masks deploy, put your own mask over your face before helping those around you) and getting a stable base of income, and then using that stable base to build momentum, generate additional support and resources, and provide low-cost or free trainings when you don't need to worry for one minute how many people participate *because you are already taken care of*.

Can you imagine how crystal clear the energy in those programs, books, podcasts, livestreams, etc. will feel when there's nothing you need to get out of them because your business is so rock solid that you can simply show up and serve because it brings you joy to offer them? And can you then imagine how people participating in those other "accessible" offers will be able to get to know you and your work and then feel drawn to invest in other containers, thus building even more momentum in your business?

MYTH #5: I'm worried that if I raise my prices, my current clients won't be able to afford me. I don't want to leave them without being helped.

This is a phase almost everyone I work with goes through, and it's really normal and understandable to be concerned about it. What you have to be careful about with this kind of question is the underlying "savior" consciousness that may be at play here. Many coaches and healer types can fall into this consciousness from time to time because of childhood programming and empathic tendencies that originated from some early childhood development wounding. Consult your therapist about that piece. But here is what I will say on the business side of things: Healthy business owners and leaders trust that everyone will be just fine. We trust that everyone is highly capable and not in need of saving. Everyone will be served, and everyone will be taken care of because there's a customer and market at every price point.

Your job as the leader is to focus on your business, which is your side of the street, and establish where you're going to play in a market since there is ample opportunity to position at any level. What works best for you? Choose that price. Because you can't serve at your highest if you're not well nourished and well compensated for your work. Then your current clients, in their sovereignty and self-capability, will be able to decide whether they want to stay working with you or if they will flow to another resource that meets their needs. Trust them to meet their own needs and trust yourself to meet your own needs.

Undoubtedly, you will have current clients who will choose to not afford you and will choose to go elsewhere. That's perfect. Every time you uplevel in your business, you will go through "client sheddings," where old or unaligned clients will move in a different direction and clear space for new clients to come in. There may be a void here where you'll be required to hold the vision, hold your commitment to yourself and the decisions you're making for the greater good of your business, and stay steady until the external circumstances catch up to reflect what you have internally decided is right for you.

> HEALTHY BUSINESS OWNERS AND LEADERS TRUST THAT EVERYONE WILL BE JUST FINE. WE TRUST THAT EVERYONE IS HIGHLY CAPABLE AND NOT IN NEED OF SAVING. EVERYONE WILL BE SERVED, AND EVERYONE WILL BE TAKEN CARE OF BECAUSE THERE'S A CUSTOMER AND MARKET AT EVERY PRICE POINT.

MYTH #6: I'm still doing healing work in the area I want to coach in. How can I help others if I'm still working on myself?

Can you see this as an asset rather than a fault? Can you see how being immersed in the work you do from an embodied place as a student of life and a never-ending seeker and experimenter in this particular field makes you an even better teacher because of your passion for the learning and growth yourself?

I coach on business, and I'm far from having everything figured out in my business. And I don't need to be in order to be an asset to you and the clients I serve, and neither do you. I'm highly invested in my growth and learning new strategies, working with mentors who experience even higher levels of entrepreneurial success, studying my audience, coming up with new theories and teachings, and experimenting and innovating in my area of the market—and then teaching what I learn. I make mistakes, fall on my face, and then coach from it, helping my clients to avoid the pitfalls I tumbled into headfirst because I went first, as leaders do.

You're going first in your modality and area of expertise. You're in it up to your little nose hairs every day, all day, and that gives you real-life embodied lessons, valuable theories and ideas, and perspectives at your fingertips that are useful and beneficial to your ideal clients. Your tool belt is full, and it's fresh because you're using those tools every day.

Healing (a.k.a. the lifelong evolution, growth, and organic human maturation process) is never finished. Waiting to be "perfect" or a "finished product" is never going to happen and waiting for it to happen will never serve anyone, and I know you don't want that.

MYTH #7: I'm worried that selling too much will come across as salesy, not to mention that it will drain my energy if I'm launching all the time.

Here's a perspective I bet most other coaches won't share with you on this: You actually need to train your audience to see you as someone to buy from, and if you don't sell enough, they will buy from someone who is selling all the time.

Read that again and let it sink in. Someone who is selling all the time is comfortable selling, and that confident vibe helps people feel comfortable buying from them in return. It's an energetic match. People want to buy from a reputable businessperson who feels confident in selling their products and services. If you're reading this and thinking that you'll just write very inspirational things and share lots of value so that when you do sell something, it'll be so rare and precious that people will fall over themselves to throw money at you because "she never sells, so I better hop on this one opportunity she's barely whispering about . . . ," let me burst that bubble for you. They won't even notice. They are going to be too busy looking at your competitors who have been rolling out consistent offers with consistent results with consistent confidence around the value all those programs bring to the people who buy them.

> YOU ACTUALLY NEED TO TRAIN YOUR AUDIENCE TO SEE YOU AS SOMEONE TO BUY FROM, AND IF YOU DON'T SELL ENOUGH, THEY WILL BUY FROM SOMEONE WHO IS SELLING ALL THE TIME.

This story also has an underlying energy and misconception that selling is taking. I see selling as giving people the opportunity to get something they want and solve a problem they don't want to have anymore and have been looking for a place to get it solved. It's win-win. Even exchange, always. The reality is that people don't get transformed by reading an inspiring Instagram post. People don't change their lives from a cool-looking infographic or a one-off livestream they watch where they "like your energy." People change their lives when they choose to make a big shift in their own behavior and get themselves into a container where they'll be taught new things and be held accountable to implementing them *over time*, and when they back their desire for change with an actual investment that puts their money where their mouth is.

ONE OF THE MANY ROLES MONEY PLAYS IN THIS SPACE IS TO REPRESENT THE DEGREE OF COMMITMENT IN TIME AND ENERGY AND SERIOUSNESS THAT SOMEONE BRINGS TO THIS PARTICULAR ISSUE. THEN THINGS START TO SHIFT. LITTLE FREEBIES AND LOW-COST PROGRAMS DO NOT HAVE THIS SAME EFFECT ON PEOPLE.

One of the many roles money plays in this space is to represent the degree of commitment in time and energy and seriousness that someone brings to this particular issue. Then things start to shift. Little freebies and low-cost programs do not have this same effect on people. When my clients decide to invest five figures and multiple five figures into themselves by enrolling in our business coaching programs, not only do they pay for the value of my mentorship and the expertise of my team and the lifetime value of the skill sets around marketing, sales, and business management that we teach that then support them to have a business that turns over multiple five- or even six-figure months *for the rest of their lives*, but they also are declaring to themselves that they are committed to growth and committed to raising the level of influence they have in their field.

Further to this, here's an example that always gets my clients laughing: Imagine that you wake up on Sunday morning craving a warm frothy **cappuccino from your favorite coffee shop.** You walk over with your honey, cozied up and ready for your favorite start to the day. When you arrive, the shop is closed, and on the door there's a sign that reads, "Sorry, we are closed today. We had a really good day yesterday, and you know, we're not about the money, and we don't want people to think we're too salesy, so please find some educational information here about the benefits and history of coffee for your enjoyment in the meantime. We'll be back when we feel the alignment is right."

YOU'D BE PISSED.

You're probably laughing right now, but why is it funny when we talk about this mindset in a coffee shop example but is somehow completely justifiable when you talk about your own business? It's not any different. Or rather, if you want to make it and be sustainable and be taken seriously in your industry and serve lots of people, it's not any different. If you're a business, you sell every day. It's your job. People *want* to buy the things you have to sell, and if you don't make it loud and clear how they can do that, you're doing them a disservice, and you're actually being selfish.

The last piece here is around how you're making launching a big deal and making it out to be something that drains your energy. This is a story you need to release. A story that is fully optional, so you don't need to buy into it any longer. We've all met that frantic coach who runs with her head cut off: "Oh, my God, I'm launching right now! Sorry I can't make dinner, or the party next week, or your baby shower the week after that. This is absolutely critical to my success and everything in my life and business hangs on this, so I have to be heads down. See you in a month." I feel so sorry for her. I used to be her. A lot of my clients used to be her until I coached them out of that nonsense.

> IF YOU'RE A BUSINESS, YOU SELL EVERY DAY. IT'S YOUR JOB. PEOPLE WANT TO BUY THE THINGS YOU HAVE TO SELL, AND IF YOU DON'T MAKE IT LOUD AND CLEAR HOW THEY CAN DO THAT, YOU'RE DOING THEM A DISSERVICE, AND YOU'RE ACTUALLY BEING SELFISH.

In my business, we make selling no big deal. I'm always launching. Not because I'm a maniac, but because all launching means is being in receiving mode. I'm offering something for people to buy and providing an opportunity for them to get support on something they need support on. That's my job. Day in and day out. I have systems around it that make it easier, of course, but the energy is what matters. It's no big deal because I decide it's no big deal, and it's really not. If one product I launch doesn't work or doesn't get the sign-ups I wanted, does it mean anything about me? Nope. I'll launch it again the next day. I'll create something else and sell that instead. I'm in this for the long haul, and one isolated event does not predict my future, establish anything about the kind of business I have or will have, or say something about my character as an entrepreneur. It's one of hundreds of things I'll feel called to create and offer to the world, and the results will vary over time, as things go. No big deal. I'm committed to my vision. I invite you into this vibe to see how it can make selling not only easier but actually fun and nourishing as well.

MYTH #8: It's a waste of time for me to put out content on Facebook or Instagram because the people on there are just friends from my old workplace and my hometown. Fred from middle school isn't going to buy life coaching from me. Where should I post instead?

If you haven't been posting somewhere for several months consistently with top-notch marketing and messaging and an offer that's proven by your market research to be desired in the market, then you can't say anything about whether your ideal audience is on that platform. There are many truths here.

First, most of my clients got their first clients from their personal network. That's right, when Fred from middle school sees you sharing on social media, offering something desirable that relates to his problems and desires, *and* he has the context of knowing you firsthand and witnessing your transformation, even from afar, he becomes the perfect potential client. You have the trust factor with Fred and every other person you're currently underestimating in your network because you have history together. You don't need strangers to buy your coaching. The reality is, those closest to you will likely be the ones most interested at first until you build more momentum in colder audiences.

Second, it's literally your job as a coach to see the best in your potential clients and to believe in people. Being judgmental about the people in your audience is the perfect way to repel potential clients because if you don't see them as highly capable and working toward evolving themselves, then you won't be a match to coach them in the first place. Try assuming the best of all people, especially the people in your current audience, and then watch what magic happens (by the way, no one comes in with a perfect audience full of potential buyers—buyers emerge when you show up powerfully and consistently). Would you be drawn to work with someone who silently thought you were a loser or not interested in improving your life or assumed you didn't have money to invest in your own growth because you weren't making an executive income? No.

> IT'S LITERALLY YOUR JOB AS A COACH TO SEE THE BEST IN YOUR POTENTIAL CLIENTS AND TO BELIEVE IN PEOPLE. BEING JUDGMENTAL ABOUT THE PEOPLE IN YOUR AUDIENCE IS THE PERFECT WAY TO REPEL POTENTIAL CLIENTS BECAUSE IF YOU DON'T SEE THEM AS HIGHLY CAPABLE AND WORKING TOWARD EVOLVING THEMSELVES, THEN YOU WON'T BE A MATCH TO COACH THEM IN THE FIRST PLACE. TRY ASSUMING THE BEST OF ALL PEOPLE, ESPECIALLY THE PEOPLE IN YOUR CURRENT AUDIENCE, AND THEN WATCH WHAT MAGIC HAPPENS.

Last, you go first. As the leader of the business, you share, offer, and teach first. You don't wait for some outside evidence, whether you determine that by the number of likes or the demographic of people in your audience and all your projections around that, to give you the blessing to go ahead and post and get advance confirmation that it's going to be well received and clients are going to fall from the sky. Think again. You start by sharing about the topic you feel called to share about, even when no one is listening. You start by offering the program you feel called to offer, even when nobody's buying. You start by putting your ideas out there, even when no one is asking you for them. Entrepreneurship, especially coaching, is a self-appointed job. You make up your title, you make up your products, you make up your entire business because you decide so. Because you feel called. And then you hold the vision until the people come. You don't try to poke your head out from behind the curtain to count how many heads are in the audience before you get on stage. You get on stage, you deliver the performance of your life, every night, until the theater is full and people are screaming "encore!" You don't get that before you give it your all first. And this is the new paradigm, my love, so the whole world and every platform is your stage.

YOU HOLD THE VISION UNTIL THE PEOPLE COME. YOU DON'T TRY TO POKE YOUR HEAD OUT FROM BEHIND THE CURTAIN TO COUNT HOW MANY HEADS ARE IN THE AUDIENCE BEFORE YOU GET ON STAGE. YOU GET ON STAGE, YOU DELIVER THE PERFORMANCE OF YOUR LIFE, EVERY NIGHT, UNTIL THE THEATER IS FULL AND PEOPLE ARE SCREAMING "ENCORE!" YOU DON'T GET THAT BEFORE YOU GIVE IT YOUR ALL FIRST.

MYTH #9: My audience is teeny tiny. I have no email list and I get like ten likes on my Instagram account. How can I build a business that supports me the way I want to be supported when I'm such small potatoes? My goals seem so far away!

No one is born with a following unless you are a Kardashian. We all start from zero. No one you look up to online started with an email list. At one point, your social media heroes also got ten likes on their posts. What did they do? They got to where they are today because they didn't care, and they kept posting anyway.

The vibe I invite you into on this is: Take one step at a time and trust that it all adds up. Every piece you write, every time you hit "publish," every time one person says yes, every client who graduates and leaves a positive testimonial, every podcast interview you get invited to do, every livestream you do when you don't feel like anyone's watching, every sales call you book, everything, absolutely everything matters, and it all adds up for you. There's no secret and there's no shortcut except to keep doing what you feel called and committed to do.

My Facebook group, Soul-Level Shifts, has almost 2,000 entrepreneurs in it today. It's incredibly active and has a wonderful energy inside. (You can join us there if you haven't already. The link is at the end of the book and on my website.) It started out with me and my VA and a few friends. It was absolute crickets for months. I built it one post at a time. One free training at a time that funneled people in. One email at a time that reminded people to join. Every little mention that I'll never know how many people saw and acted on. Even now, sometimes it goes quiet in the group, and I have to reinvest some time and energy into rekindling the conversation. That's how it goes. And in a few years, I'm confident there will be 20,000 or more people inside, but I'm not going to be upset because we're not *there* yet, I'm going to nurture who is there now and give them my all.

Nurture who is there with you now. Have ten followers? Then imagine those ten people sitting in your living room. How would you show up for them, sitting live right in front of you looking right into your eyes? Want 100,000 followers? Then how would you show up and talk and move if you already had those numbers? Do that now and you'll be a match to have them eventually, as you grow.

> WANT 100,000 FOLLOWERS? THEN HOW WOULD YOU SHOW UP AND TALK AND MOVE IF YOU ALREADY HAD THOSE NUMBERS? DO THAT NOW AND YOU'LL BE A MATCH TO HAVE THEM EVENTUALLY, AS YOU GROW.

Truly, an empire is built one day at a time, day after day.

MYTH #10: I don't want to make a million dollars. I'd be happy with just $5K/month so I could live independently of any job. A million-dollar business sounds like too much work.

Again, I'm not here to convince you to make a certain amount of money. Your desires are up to you. What I am here to do is point out when you're telling stories or settling for less than simply what's available to you at no sacrifice or additional cost. What I know for certain from running a business that was barely getting by at $5K/month and doing everything myself because I didn't have the resources to hire support versus running a business that makes $100K/month with a lot of structure and support that exists outside of me (and watching dozens of my clients uplevel along the same lines) is that it is far easier and more enjoyable to be running the latter. Contrary to what you might think if you do the math and reckon that the amount of hard work you put in to run a business at $5K/month is simply multiplied times twenty to go to six-figure months. The math doesn't work like that, not by a long shot.

You'll never work harder than when you're earning under $20K/month. A higher income bracket means less work because you have more people to help you run the business. It means more time working exclusively in your zone of genius and allowing others to handle the other parts of the job. It means the time you spend in the business is actually more nourishing, you feel less on your own, and you have overflow, which means money left over to put into investments that grow your net worth. This way you'll have *money working for you* instead of you working for money, which is how the wealthy mindset around money and investment works.

If you stick with earning the bare minimum, which will barely cover rent, food, travel, and incidentals plus a very meager savings, you're setting yourself to run on the hamster wheel your whole life instead of building something sustainable that relies on more than just you, meaning its weight is distributed among the hands and brains of many and reaches far more people than you'd be capable of doing on your own playing small. The choice is yours.

MYTH #11: I know money won't make me happy, so I don't want to focus on that. I want to have more free time and energy to do the things I love and travel and be free, etc. Money will just get in the way and distract me from what's really important.

Quick answer: Why would you not just have both? Have more money *and* more time and energy to do whatever you want. See the explanation above in Myth #10. More money actually provides the means to free up your time and energy and do more of what makes you happy. Any illusion of having to choose is optional, and one quick mindset fix away.

Long answer: No, money won't make you happy. There's no direct correlation. It won't bring you happiness and it won't take you away from happiness (or it doesn't have to, as you can choose differently). Money will only magnify who you already are and open doors, provide opportunities, give you more choices, and put the world at your fingertips. I'll say yes to that any day. Money is neutral and fundamentally functions as an extension of your power and will in the world, meaning it amplifies your influence and power to get things done however you see fit. And because I'm guessing you're a really good-hearted person reading this book, you'll do good things with it. You can use it as you like, and your happiness is up to you.

Any false trade-off you see between money and happiness or money and freedom or money and being a good person is black-and-white thinking and is creating false dichotomies where none need to exist. Any idea that money comes as a cost versus a natural extension of your putting your work out into the world in the way you were always intended to and choosing that you can have both wealth and wellness is simply a story, and one that you are in charge of disproving and finding evidence to the contrary. Be wildly wealthy *and* independently happy; be of great service *and* greatly compensated. No choice or trade-off required.

BE WILDLY WEALTHY AND INDEPENDENTLY HAPPY; BE OF GREAT SERVICE AND GREATLY COMPENSATED. NO CHOICE OR TRADE-OFF REQUIRED.

MYTH #12: There are so many people in need in the world. How can I feel good about getting rich and doing well for myself when there are so many people struggling?

The simple answer is that you'll never get poor enough to help the poorest people become rich. You'll be in a much better position to help more people, donate powerfully to the causes you care about, and back well-established organizations doing widespread good work in the world if you come in with money of your own. Money is required to build schools and homes, put food on the table, fly in aid, support political causes that will change the way things are done, feed hungry animals, and more. Become abundantly well resourced, in charge of assets that stabilize your own wealth (like a well-run business, real estate, and other long-term investments), then move from that place of wellness and overflow and allow your money to have a ripple effect far beyond you into the world, as you desire.

Let's think about it this way: Although perhaps a natural human reaction, would feeling guilty about being healthy when you walk through a cancer ward serve you or any patient there? Or would it be a better use of your health to smile and hold the hands of the patients *and* then mobilize behind causes that can cure disease? Is it a good use of your energy to feel guilty about your power and opportunity, or is it a better use of what's been provided to you to wildly succeed, set an example for others as inspiration, and share your wealth with many more? P.S. Beware of the savior consciousness, as discussed earlier in this chapter. You're also allowed to enjoy your money and not feel guilty about that either.

> IS IT A GOOD USE OF YOUR ENERGY TO FEEL GUILTY ABOUT YOUR POWER AND OPPORTUNITY, OR IS IT A BETTER USE OF WHAT'S BEEN PROVIDED TO YOU TO WILDLY SUCCEED, SET AN EXAMPLE FOR OTHERS AS INSPIRATION, AND SHARE YOUR WEALTH WITH MANY MORE?

HOMEWORK FOR THIS CHAPTER

1. Which myth did you most closely identify with from this chapter? Write about how you were thinking about it before versus what you know to be true now and what you're *choosing* to be true for you now.

2. What did I say here that triggered you the most? Why might that be exactly the thing that needs to shift for you to hit the next big level you're desiring?

3. Write down one big takeaway from this chapter and exactly how you're bringing that into your business today. Commit to three small changes you can make right now based on what you learned here.

CONCLUSION

BALI, INDONESIA
MARCH 14, 2022
8:32 A.M.

Nearly every morning, I swing open my huge wooden front door and there's an older Balinese woman walking down my driveway with a tray of offerings stacked generously on one hand. She kneels down in front and waves a single stick of incense into the morning air, gently placing a tiny woven tray of flowers, rice, candies, and incense on the ground.

To me, the offerings are a reminder that the locals know they are cocreating their reality with support from the gods, their ancestors, and nature itself—cosmically interwoven with forces they cannot see or control, blindly trusting that acknowledging and dancing with these forces will be beneficial to them. Unsurprisingly, I've landed here because I resonate with their way of doing things. I wouldn't be here doing what I do without the unseen support of a lot of other beings on this planet and well beyond.

I've been in Bali for four years to the day as I write this final chapter, and I'll never tire of the ceremonies, the sweet smell of the damp air, and how I get to walk barefoot on the earth every single day. I am more connected to the elements here than I ever have been anywhere else. Each morning the roosters crow, the insects rattle, the frogs croak, the dogs bark, and I step out into the full buzz of aliveness of this island I've chosen to call home. I look around at my beautiful villa with its white walls and Javanese-style wooden pillars, at my furry whiskered angels, and at the palm trees draping their branches over the water in my pool that glistens invitingly in the morning sun.

For some people, the journey of finding home is as simple as being born in one place and never leaving. For others, like myself, it takes a quarter of a lifetime to wander the earth and search inside the nooks and crevices of endless foreign cultures, trying them on like sunglasses in the mirror, squinting and trying to see which one suits best.

"Where do I belong?" is a question that didn't come with an easy answer for me.

"Where is home for you?" people ask me in Bali today, expecting me to say "America" or some faraway place where I look like I come from. But I answer: "Here."

When I bought my first one-way ticket from Hawaii to Bali, I was burned out from the years of living out of a suitcase and moving to countries like Nigeria, Ethiopia, and Mongolia every three months. I set the intention to finally find a home and had an inkling it might be in Bali, where all those cool Instagram influencers, digital nomads, and free spirits were living.

I wanted so badly to be like them. I figured if I breathed the same air as them in their coworking spaces, I, too, might be able to make a living off my laptop and say goodbye forever to living between two states of permanent scarcity: scrounging by to save up corporate money and scrounging by to live off corporate money.

My Instagram feed on March 14, 2018, is a picture of a traditional Balinese *joglo*. The caption reads, "Home for the next couple of months."

I had no idea.

I fell in love, hard. I found a community where I can pick up a conversation like long-lost friends with anyone in any room. I found deep familiarity with the land, the ceremonies, and the energy of Ubud. Since then, I've found my purpose. I started a business. I met a man and fell in love. I bought a home. I built another home. I broke up with said man. I wrote a book.

Today I run a multi-seven-figure company that serves hundreds of people, and I manage a team of eight amazing humans who all support this purpose—a purpose I couldn't see for miles when I got here. A purpose that was shrouded in so much healing work I needed to do. Healing that Bali brought to my heart and my body. Healing that my community and friends have witnessed. Chapters that have opened and closed on this island.

Those of you who know Bali know how time works here: It doesn't exist. It speeds up, it slows down, and it goes in spirals. Four years have felt like four lifetimes.

I bow onto this land today and give thanks; I give my humble prayers for the grace this place has shown me.

It amazes me that I moved here with the intention to monetize my blog or to find a simple way to make a few thousand dollars per month from my laptop so I could stay as long as I wanted. I am still, at heart, a dedicated world citizen and spiritual seeker, and the business has its origins in simply wanting to support those parts of me without having to answer to anyone else. I longed to be able to pick up my life and sit on the banks of the Ganges River in India with my palms face up, my face smiling into the Himalayan mountains whenever I wanted. I knew I had to be able to fly to Beijing and walk through the street markets chatting in Mandarin with the old men selling *chuan'r* or walk through a chilly mountain down in northern Peru prepping for a multiday hike in the Andes. I had to be free to go when Nepal called or when the Amazon wanted me back.

I think it was in part the sheer innocence and purity of my desire and my "why" behind starting my business that led it to become so much more than that. I've been awakened, polished, and healed by way of growing a multimillion-dollar company. It's led me home, opened my heart, brought me love and a chosen family, and it's been the greatest spiritual awakening I've ever had.

Turns out I didn't need to go to the ashram every year, I could simply run a business in a conscious way. Turns out becoming a self-made, heart-led entrepreneur is one of the ultimate paths of spiritual healing and personal growth I could have ever dreamed up.

It has also, as I intended, put the world at my fingertips.

I remember walking through the luxurious Palm Jumeirah in Dubai a few months ago and striking up a conversation with the Italian owner of the restaurant where I stopped to eat at sunset and watch the city sparkle from a distance. Despite living in one of the most cosmopolitan cities in the world, this man didn't want to be there. He'd accidentally landed in Dubai after a friend invited him for vacation one year, then settled into the comfortable predictability of a "good enough" salary running his buddy's restaurant and had begrudgingly stayed for the six years since.

Six years?! I choked on my gelato. *How could anyone stay in one place for so long, no less a place they don't even love being? Don't they realize how free they could actually be?*

Don't they want to choose to be somewhere that lights every cell of their body on fire each day, or at the very least feels like their true and chosen home?

But yes, you'd have to become self-made, emancipated from any paycheck, and fully untethered from any one single place on earth to get the all-access pass to the freedom, abundance, and joy that is your birthright. You'd have to choose the path of becoming an entrepreneur and declare yourself economically independent from the large corporations and usual suspects who hand out financial rations and keep you small.

You'd have to take the risks, understand your genius, monetize your God-given gifts, heal your childhood wounds, stand up as a leader, and open your heart to the wildness and richness of the journey itself. You'd have to bet on yourself and play to win, over and over again. Be unafraid of reinventing yourself, of starting something new, of building from the ground up as many times as it takes because you know who *you* are.

You'd have to look fear and failure in the face every day and embrace it until you meet the fierce, bold, unshakable leader within. You'd have to surrender into the unknown again and again, trust yourself fully, and cocreate with your cosmic and universal support system.

That's why you hold this book in your hands.

Because you were born to be self-made.

You were born with the desire, the faint knowing that perhaps has grown so loud that it pounds deafeningly in your ears. It won't go away until you follow the voice and follow your sacred yes, no matter how bewildering the guidance is, and leap into the void.

You may get to this point in the book and say, "Okay, Elaina, this has all been great and inspiring, but I'm still not *there* yet," wherever "there" is for you. There's a significant next level awaiting you that you had in mind when you picked up this book: a new stage of life, a new income level, a new chapter of your business perhaps, and it's not here yet for you.

This, my friend, is the whole point.

If you take away anything from this book, let it be this: Who you are, who you're becoming, and who you're meant to be is created in the spaces in between. The void we spoke of in

> WHO YOU ARE, WHO YOU'RE BECOMING, AND WHO YOU'RE MEANT TO BE IS CREATED IN THE SPACES IN BETWEEN.

Chapter One. The space in between, where, how fittingly, I'm leaving you off as we part ways: between soul mates, adjusting to singlehood, taking a good look in the mirror and seeing who the heck I became in this last relationship and who I want to be in the next one. Is there any certainty of me finding love again? No, not in a practical sense (and, God, let's not speak of any statistics characterizing the dating market for women in their thirties), but we know I've never lived a very practical, reasonable, logical life. My next great love is not here yet, but I feel it in my bones. I know it's coming by faith and faith alone, choosing to believe that although there may be space in between the conventional life highlights, there's no space between my destiny and my desires, nor between yours. I choose to believe that what I desire is my destiny, and choose to not question, fear, or doubt whether what I see in the innermost chambers of my heart is a premonition of what's to come.

I believe that who you are in these spaces in between is the most important thing of all. Who are you when you're sitting there staring at a lack of money, a lack of partner, a lack of clients, a lack of health, a lack of energy, a lack of community, a lack of home? Who are you when what you dearly want isn't here yet or when it doesn't look like it's going to happen at all? Can you and do you choose to hold the faith and the vision and lead yourself through the abyss to the other side? How do you speak to yourself in these moments? What are your thoughts like? Do you still back yourself unconditionally and show up with the same kind of support you'd show up with for a client in the same situation?

Who you choose to become in each moment is what dictates the trajectory of how your life unfolds. What's possible for me is possible for you, even after taking into account all the reasons why things shouldn't be stacked in your favor. Even when the circumstances and hard evidence would indicate otherwise. You don't need to be special to achieve this level of success or to live the lifestyle of your dreams. You simply need to be deeply aligned and available for exactly what you desire along with heaping doses of courage, deep self-belief, and a micro dose of sheer delusional insanity that what you desire is possible for you—then it's just a matter of *when,* not *if* it happens for you too.

***

As I sit here now, I watch my two kitties chasing dragonflies in the morning sun, as free and wild as they were born to be. I hear the faint temple music and the birds singing the Balinese gospel hymn. The offerings sit lovingly on my doorstep, now covered in ants that come to lick the flowers and eat the sweets and take it all back to nature.

The spirit world is very alive and palpable here, and I love living in a culture that honors and includes the unseen realms of support we have available to us. I wouldn't be here without interweaving myself with that supernatural support system.

Living in such a rich foreign culture reminds me every single day of the culture I feel called to create and participate in on this planet—one where all humans do the work they were born to do. Where every person, should they have the desire and should they choose to accept the mission, be able to walk the Earth and share their magic freely while being compensated abundantly for their gifts. Where our most precious, nonrenewable resource is kept sacred: our time.

My biggest wish for you is that you become the chief executive officer of your *time* for the rest of your life. And that you become the chief energetic officer of the quality of life you wish to lead.

Be unwavering and uncompromising in how you want to spend your days while you're here with us. Set yourself up for a life of abundance in energy, freedom, community, and, yes, lots of money too, so that you may have the resources at your fingertips to use your time more wisely and with more joy, able to opt into the fullness of the experiences available on this planet.

May the journey of becoming self-made bolster your soul, heal your heart, and free your gifts.

May the journey itself be so nourishing, challenging, and empowering for you that someday you look back and laugh about how you accidentally became a multimillionaire and changed thousands of lives while you were merely skipping down the road, arms linked with some amazing people, fully absorbed in the thrill of each moment, fully absorbed in your creation as it was coming to life and becoming larger than life.

Here's to you—your success, your larger-than-life visions, your soul expansion, and your gifts shining and changing the world. Here's to you becoming self-made.

Elaina Ray

ACKNOWLEDGMENTS

I'll never forget my thirty-second birthday on September 16, 2021, when I sat in a sister circle with a handful of girlfriends, all of whom reflected to me that this was indeed the year to fulfill my lifelong dream of writing a book.

One month later, I was mulling over ideas on what on Earth to actually write a book about when the idea dawned on me to simply write to my former self, the version of me five years ago who was clueless about how to turn her dream into a business and sustainable life path, and to share everything I wished I had known then. To write to the version of me who didn't believe she could even consider becoming an *entrepreneur*. This idea made me burst into wild, sobbing tears and I knew in my heart of aligned hearts that this was the book.

Four months later, I plopped the completed manuscript down on the virtual desk of my publishing house, proud as I'd ever been of anything.

I have many people to thank for this creative feat of bringing my life's work to date to the page.

First of all, a giant thank-you to all of my current Elaina Ray team: Hannah Gorvin, Lois Mckenzie, Kayla Yoder, Jesse Noemind, Cait Rose, Rickilee Walls, Lauren Megan, and Taryn Raine. I couldn't do what I do without you. You amaze me by always being two steps ahead of me, and I'm immensely grateful for your unwavering patience, for turning the chaos into order, and for sharing your brilliance with me and all of our clients and community. You share my passion for this mission and have shown me how possible it is for me to feel held, supported, and seen behind the scenes. Through you, I learned that I don't have to do this alone, and that it's far more enriching, in fact, to do it together. Each of you is ridiculously talented and powerful, and I'm deeply honored that you choose to work with me and our clients. I also wouldn't have had the spaciousness to write this book in just four months without you.

Thank you to the YGTMedia Publishing Team: Sabrina Greer, Christine Stock, my editor Tania Moraes-Vaz, and Doris Chung and others behind the scenes, all of whom spent countless hours going back and forth over cover photo options, editing this book down to the very last comma, and helping me stay on track to publish it on a tight deadline while running a company, building a house, going through a heart-wrenching breakup, and traveling the world all at the same time. I had long lists of recommended publishers from friends but hired you on complete blind faith and intuition because you just felt good to my system and my heart simply said yes. It was the best decision I could have made for my first book baby. Thank you for making this possible.

Thank you to the coaches who have had an incredible, life-changing impact on my work and the way I see the world. Just to name a few: Cait Scudder, Emily Utter, Juliana Garcia, Katrina Ruth, and Amanda Frances. I am honored to have been your student and client at one time or another and your words still echo positively in my mind today. Thank you to my primary healers and therapists who have supported my body and mind to come along on this wild ride with me and to be able to hold it all: Phill Hunt, Nigel McFarland, and Terye Trombley.

Thank you to my Bali team who care for my home and personal life: Gusti, Trisna, Komang, and Kadek. You bless my life with so much ease, grace, and more support than I could have ever dreamed of having. I am grateful to see your smiles every single day.

Thank you, Mama Bali, for allowing me to make my home on your land. I am blessed from many lifetimes to be able to be here. I have been healed, upgraded, and uplifted by being here. Your people, your soil, and your culture have been the medicine my soul was yearning for. I've felt at home since the very first time I set foot on this precious island. I pray for your blessing and permission to continue to build my life here.

And last but definitely not least, thank you dearly to my beloved parents, Rita and Robert Giolando, for the lifelong encouragement to write a book and for the childhood imprint you gave me that allowed me to believe I can truly do anything. Thank you to my countless friends and chosen family here in Bali who supported me through the ups and downs of the writing process, especially during my season of unimaginable heartache. Thank you to my client community and social media audience who cheered me on from the inception of this idea to its final launch date. I truly love you. I am honored and overjoyed that I could have created a business based on simply serving and forming genuine relationships with my favorite people on the planet.

From the bottom of my heart, I love what I do and who I've gotten to become along the way.

RESOURCES & WORKS CITED

WORKS CITED

1. McKay, Matt. "Entrepreneur vs. Employee: Three Big Differences in Your Personal Finances." McKay Wealth Management, November 13, 2017. https://www.mckaywealthgroup.com/entrepreneur-vs-employee-three-big-differences-personal-finances/.

2. Post, Special to Financial. "Fulfillment Equals Productivity for Millennials at Work." financialpost. Financial Post, February 1, 2016. https://financialpost.com/executive/careers/fulfillment-equals-productivity-for-millennials-at-work.

3. Carter, Timothy. "The True Failure Rate of Small Businesses." Entrepreneur. Entrepreneur, December 23, 2020. https://www.entrepreneur.com/article/361350.

4. Zimmerman, Eilene. "Only 2% of Women-Owned Businesses Break the $1 Million Mark -- Here's How to Be One of Them." Forbes. Forbes Magazine, July 1, 2015. https://www.forbes.com/sites/eilenezimmerman/2015/04/01/only-2-of-women-owned-businesses-break-the-1-million-mark-heres-how-to-be-one-of-them/?sh=7007cf6127a6.

5. Loudenback, Tanza. "Experts Say 95% of Money Advice Focuses on the Wrong Thing." Business Insider. Business Insider, March 11, 2019. https://www.businessinsider.com/personal-finance/increase-income-or-cut-expenses-financial-planner-2019-3.

INSPIRATIONAL QUOTES

Chris Harder: https://www.facebook.com/chriswharder

Wayne Dyer: https://www.youtube.com/watch?v=XicKygU-g1s

MASTERCLASSES AND COURSES

PRICING: Check out the *Aligned Premium Pricing* masterclass on elainaray.com if pricing your offers is something with which you're still struggling. This masterclass has helped hundreds of entrepreneurs to naturally and effortlessly land on a price that feels good for them and their audience.

NICHING: If deciding on your niche and creating your first offer is proving challenging for you, you're not alone and don't have to stay stuck trying to figure it out on your own. Check out my best-selling *Signature Offers That Sell* course that is designed to walk you through every step from the general idea of wanting to be a coach to putting together an offer you're obsessed with, from finding ready-to-invest, ideal clients for that offer to getting the foundation of your business rock solid and scalable up to six figures per year. It's everything I would do from start to finish in just ten easy modules if I were starting my business over from scratch, and it's helped hundreds of people just like you to get the clarity you need to move forward and have the impact and income you desire.

MANIFESTING: If you want to watch me teach live about my manifestation of partnership and how love, money, and business are all interconnected, check out my *Attracting Big Love & Money* masterclass on my website.

WANT TO DIVE DEEPER?

Find more resources related to the book that will help you grow your business at elainaray.com/becomingselfmade.

You can also download our most up-to-date free trainings at elainaray.com/freegifts.

Connect with me on Instagram @heyelainaray or by joining our private Facebook group, Soul-Level Shifts at facebook.com/groups/soullevelshifts.

I look forward to connecting with you and witnessing you on your own incredible journey of becoming self-made.

Love,
Elaina

YGTMedia Co. is a blended boutique publishing house for mission-driven humans. We help seasoned and emerging authors "birth their brain babies" through a supportive and collaborative approach. Specializing in narrative nonfiction and adult and children's empowerment books, we believe that words can change the world, and we intend to do so one book at a time.

🌐 ygtmedia.co/publishing

📷 @ygtmedia.company

ⓕ @ygtmedia.co